Great Britain and Ireland

Short Stay Guide

Great Britain and Ireland

 Little Hills Press

Text by Fay Smith and LHP Editorial Staff
© Little Hills Press, February 2002

Editor and designer: Mark Truman
Publisher: Charles Burfitt

Printed in China

Great Britain and Ireland
Short Stay Guide
ISBN 1 86315 197 4

Little Hills Press
Sydney, Australia
www.littlehills.com
info@littlehills.com

DISCLAIMER
Whilst all care has been taken by the publisher and authors to ensure that the information is accurate and up to date, the publisher does not take responsibility for the information published herein or the consequences of its use. The recommendations are those of the writing team, and as things get better or worse, with places closing and others opening, some elements in the book may be inaccurate when you arrive. Please inform us of any discrepancies so that we can update subsequent editions.

Little Hills™ and are registered trademarks of Little Hills Press Pty Ltd.

Contents

Part Three

Preface

WELCOME TO GREAT BRITAIN AND IRELAND! These amazing countries are made up of many landscapes, each with its own particular identity. Every city and town has a rich history and will provide you with unique experiences never to be forgotten.

Great Britain and Ireland conjure images of lush rolling hills and great medieval monuments. London, a metropolis of 7 million people, has its historical Westminster Abbey, the once-insidious Tower of London, the royal residence of Buckingham Palace, the British Museum and its wealth of possessions, and the extravagant Harrods department store. In the north of England, York's medieval walls recall its Roman and Anglo-Saxon heritage, while the huge York Minster is resplendent with wonderful Gothic architecture. Visitors to The Lake District can walk through the beautiful countryside that inspired Wordsworth. Manchester is a tough and gritty city of industry, with row houses lining its streets, and plenty of museums to explore. Chester is a quaint city in midwestern England which displays its links to the Roman Empire in the Grosvenor Museum. In Stratford-upon-Avon, visitors wander through the birthplace of the world's most famous poet and playwright, murmuring well known lines spoken by Hamlet, Macbeth, young Romeo and many others. The riverside institutions of Oxford and Cambridge boast magnificent architecture and future Nobel Prize winners (together they have educated more than 100 to date). Bath's Museum of Costume and its ancient Roman relaxation centre draw in the crowds, who generally take a trip to the mysterious neolithic site of Stonehenge nearby.

Edinburgh is a vibrant cultural centre overlooked by its panoramic castle. In Glasgow, Scotland's largest city, you can explore Bothwell castle and the impressive collection in the Hunterian Museum and Art Gallery. Northern Ireland's Belfast has crept back onto traveller's itineraries in recent years.

Dublin's Trinity College houses that survivor of the Dark Ages, the elaborate Book of Kells, and visitors to the city can also enjoy a pint at the Guiness Brewery, or trace the footsteps of the pioneer of modern prose, James Joyce. The riverside tranquility of Cork, its bustling nightlife and nearby Blarney castle, make this city worth a stop. The Dingle Peninsula, on Ireland's southwest coast, has a plethora of arch-aeological treasures, medieval buildings and scenic vistas. The Aran Islands, off Galway, entice visitors with the raw and rugged beauty of their soaring cliffs and imposing ancient forts.

There is a place in Great Britain and Ireland to appeal to every traveller.

This book is designed for people who plan to visit particular cities and regions, whether or not they are on a whirlwind tour. It assumes that you do not have a lot of time in these places, and provides thorough details of their main attractions so that you can head directly to the spots that interest you most. It therefore lists what are in our opinion the most important sights to see.

Others may prefer to rise in the morning at their leisure, spend some time getting to know the local scene, the people and the attractions, then find their favourite restaurant, club or park, or a delightful little bookshop where they can browse endlessly. The pace of your holiday is completely dependent on you.

We have developed suggested tours for you to undertake on foot. Whilst exploring Great Britains's cities and towns, cars are really an encumberance, even in a vast city such as London, where it is best to take advantage of the trains and then hail a cab if necessary. Going on foot with a light rucksack means that you are more flexible and can adapt your plans without unnecessary hassles, such as finding parking, paying for parking, having to return to the car constantly whenever you wish to move on, and worrying about it being broken into or damaged while you are away.

How To Use This Book

Symbols

Throughout the text you will find that symbols have been used to denote the information that follows, whether it be an admission price, opening time, phone number, email or web address. This will aid you in locating the specific details you desire more quickly.

Here is a list of the symbols used with an explanation of each:

    ℡ indicates a phone number

    ✪ indicates a price

    🕐 indicates opening times

    👁 indicates a web site

    ✗ indicates an email address

Accommodation and Eating Out

The *Accommodation* and *Food and Drink* sections contain by no means an exhaustive list of what each city has to offer. We have tried to cater for a range of tastes and provide suggestions for your selection. Places listed are designed to give you a basis for comparison and to act at the very least as a starting point for the planning of your holiday. All budgets from lavish to limited have been considered and included.

Taxes

Where possible we have included the tax for a specific service within Great Britain and Ireland. For example, a 17.5% VAT is included in the price of most consumables. In restaurants a 10-15% tip is expected if a service fee is not already charged. Cab drivers in London normally receive 10% on top of the fare.

Maps

Before you begin your trip, we suggest that you purchase comprehensive maps of the cities you intend to visit - ones that include as much detail of the streets, avenues and alleys as possible. Guidebooks, because of space restrictions, usually provide less detail and seek to give visitors their bearings and a general overview of the city's layout. For the serious traveller, such maps will not suffice and shouldn't be relied upon. In a foreign city you want to be able to pinpoint your location as accurately as possible, to improve your sightseeing efficiency and to ensure that you do not miss anything. A good map will also come in handy if you find yourself a little lost after an intrepid stroll. In addition, if you plan to tour an entire country, perhaps by car, a thorough road map is essential.

Internet Information

For your convenience you will find throughout this book relevant websites and email addresses, which can be used for the preliminary planning of your holiday in Great Britain and Ireland.

PART ONE

Introduction

T HIS CHAPTER OUTLINES some travel tips which you may find helpful. Specific details for each city or town, including local transport, shopping, accommodation, food and sightseeing, are contained in each section devoted to the particular areas we have covered.

Passport

You need a passport to travel. For first time travellers the following are some of the documents required before you can be issued with a passport - birth certificate and/or proof of citizenship, photographs of which at least two are passport-size, your drivers' license and so on. Normally you will have a face-to-face interview with a government official.

Generally speaking you are looking at paying over A$130 (US$65) for a passport valid for 10 years. In most cases passports are valid for 10 years, however they are useless if they have less than 6 months left on them unless you are an Australian going to New Zealand and vice versa. This does not apply to any other countries.

Here are some important contacts who will tell you exactly what you need and where to lodge the application:

Australia: ℂ131232
                  ☜www.dfat.gov.au/passports

Canada: ℂ800 567 6868
                  ☜www.dfait-maeci.gc.ca/passport/passport.htm

New Zealand: ℂ0800 225 050
                  fax 64 4 748 010
                  ☜www.passports.govt.nz/

United Kingdom: ℂ0870 521 0410
                  ☜www.ukpa.gov.uk

USA: ℂ1 900 225 5674 or 1 888 362 8668
                  ☜www.travel.state.gov

Money

Some of us still like to have a few travellers cheques just in case, however the way of the present is the credit card or the bank card, which you can activate at any ATM in most cities in Great Britain and Ireland.

If you have a credit card make sure it also has a pin number. This may seem like a superfluous comment, however some credit cards are only secured by a password, which is useless if the ATM in Great Britain requires you to enter a pin number for your card.

Make sure the account your card accesses is cashed up before you travel. Also check to see if the money is accessible before you leave, just in case the bank or the financial organisation you deal with has made a mistake or is suffering technical problems. Try making a simple withdrawal and check the balance.

You might like to get the phone numbers you will need to call if you have credit card hassles in each of the countries you plan to visit. If you want to, test them from home before you leave. At night it will probably cost you $2 in total and save you making frantic calls to dead ends in the unfortunate event that a problem arises.

Web Sites for the Major Credit Cards

These sites can provide you with the location of offices and ATMs in Great Britain and Ireland.

- www.americanexpress.com.au/atm/atm.asp
- www.thomascook.com (a confusing site but you may be able to find your way around it)
- www.mastercard.com/atm
- www.visa.com/pd/atm/main.html

When changing money at either a bank or a Bureau de Change it is important to check the commission fee to avoid being overcharged. Ask beforehand or check the notices near the counter carefully (look for the fine print!). Fees should be no more than a few pounds.

Make sure you always keep the receipts. If you are heading into Great Britain from another European country or vice versa, and you want to change your money from the currency of one country to that of your destination, you will invariably be asked to produce a receipt to prove that you purchased the currency whilst in the country you are in. If you cannot show the receipt you will be denied.

Contact Details and Valuables

The following tip is something that any travel agent and decent guidebook will advise.

It is worthwhile to have two copies of each of the documents listed on the following page.

- Passport - the front two pages which have your identification details and photograph, and also pages where Visas appear.
- Your ticket/s

Street scene in London

- Driver's license
- Insurance documentation
- Travellers Cheque numbers
- Credit Card details - just the numbers, not any identifying marks showing what card it is. Write them in a jumbled up way that doesn't look specific except to you.

Put these at the bottom of your suitcase where you will hopefully not see them until you return and unpack your bags. Forget about them for now. If you need them you will know where to find them.

Leave the second lot of copies with family back home. This will save you a lot of problems if disaster strikes.

Insurance

It is advisable to take out comprehensive insurance for the duration of your stay. Your travel agent can handle this for you and it normally covers you for loss of personal belongings, specific flight cancellations or rerouting, medical costs including all hospital and doctors' fees and any emergency transport associated with this, injury, and death (not suicide). Payment is made for the number of days you are away. Of course, the rates vary as does the coverage, so shop around.

Driving Through Great Britain and Ireland

Camper vans and mobile homes (RVs in the US) are common throughout Europe. Using one makes it obvious that you are a tourist, not only by the number plate. It is a convenient way to travel but be warned that when you leave the vehicle it can become a target for thieves, since the theory is that travelling tourists have their valuables centred in one place: the vehicle. So it is a good idea to have your passport, credit cards and money on you. Any other valuables you do not plan to take with you should be hidden somewhere in the vehicle and not exposed if someone peers through the window.

Some people opt for a van or a station wagon, in which they can put a fold-down mattress. These are not obvious tourist vehicles and so may have less chance of being tamperered with, although in some cities it is essential to hide everything from view regardless of the type of vehicle, otherwise a break-in is guaranteed.

Remember, in budgeting for travelling around, you should keep in mind the cost of fuel in your different ports of call. As a rule of thumb the country areas will be more expensive than the city. Diesel will be more expensive per gallon or litre but will take you much further per litre or gallon and is more efficient.

Trains

Britrail is one way to book and organise your tickets. It allows you to develop some flexibility with regard to where you want to travel. In addition to the basic travel component of the fare you must pay an additional charge for your individual seat. Depending on the country and the type of train, seats must be booked in advance, although this is not always necessary and you should check first.

The three web sites listed below have good information and allow you to book and pay online.

BritRail: 👁www.britrail.com

Rail Pass Express: 👁www.eurail.com

RailEurope: 👁www.raileurope.com (info and commercial)

Note that if you travel at off peak times the prices are much cheaper. This is especially the case if you book a certain number of days in advance. If you are going to be there for a week or so and plan to do a lot of travel by train, enquire at the rail information centres for their special passes giving you cheaper fares.

Taxis

Public transport in Ireland and the UK is generally good. Because of London's size, though, you may need a taxi at some stage to fill in a gap. Or you may just wish to stay out of the penetrating drizzle when you're dressed up and on your way to the theatre.

The black cabs are almost as unmistakable as the red double decker buses roaming the streets. About 23,000 operate in the city, and they are not cheap. It may make you feel better about paying high fares to know that black cab drivers in London study for two years and take a number of tough exams before they qualify to drive a taxi. In order to pass they literally have to know the city like the back of their hand, so you will get the best possible service on the quickest available route to your destination.

Fees begin at the £1.20 base and tick over at 20p per 219m travelled. There are surcharges at night, a booking fee for ordering a cab over the phone, and a 10% tip is expected on top of the fare. For women travelling alone, Lady Cabs can be contacted on ☏7254 3500.

If the London Underground is a reasonable alternative, use it.

Most taxis do not accept credit cards, so you should take it as given that cabs require cash.

It can sometimes occur that your hotel is not far from the station or airport where you have just arrived - but it is raining and the distance is too far to cart your luggage. If you are in the queue and discover that the drivers are enquiring about your destination then waving you away and moving onto the next person, it is because you do not have a decent fare to offer them. Should you find yourself in a similar situation, head into the street and hail a taxi - once you are settled comfortably inside with all your gear, break the news to the driver in a confident, matter-of-fact tone.

Force yourself to shrug off the travel fatigue and have presence of mind when you arrive in a new city. Watch what the locals are doing - it may take some minutes - but you will soon find the nearest taxi stand and line up like everyone else.

Buses

In London, the two types of buses are the famous red double deckers, and the newer, regular buses. A few things to note: sometimes you will need to flag a bus down before it stops, and have the correct change for your trip - keep some loose pennies in your pocket. Having said that, bus fares in London are simple. Journeys within the city centre are £1 and in outer London, 70p. Bus passes of varying time length are available and may be a good idea for value.

Bus services in other cities of Great Britain and Ireland are efficient and well priced.

What to Take

Great Britain and Ireland, for Australians, United States citizens from southern California and in fact anyone living below the 35th parallel, are cold and wet, particularly if you are travelling in January and February when temperatures during the day in London and Dublin normally hover below 10C and drop to freezing point at night. In summer temperatures rarely reach above 25C, but be prepared for the odd hot one.

During winter, temperatures are not likely to climb above 10C in most places, and the rain is more prolific, particularly in the north and west. Wind becomes a factor, too. More than half the days of the year are overcast, and weather has a habit of changing throughout any given day. Neither Great Britain or Ireland are subject to extreme weather. The following items are certainly essential:

- A warm overcoat.
- A water and rain resistant coat including head cover - not one that is just damp resistant.
- An umbrella that you can fold up.
- A scarf.
- A hat or beanie, preferably one that covers the ears.
- A thick jumper (pullover).
- A winter suit (if you are going on business).
- Sturdy shoes - if you have a look at what you normally wear, they are probably thin soled leather shoes, or some sort of synthetic material that is not particularly thick. You may have to invest in a pair of thick soled shoes that will have you walking a couple of extra inches off the ground. As for pricing - check locally, and also whether they are water resistant.
- Walking shoes - a comfortable pair of well cushioned walking shoes are perfect for traversing the staggering number of cobblestone streets to be found throughout Europe. Level bitumen or beautiful soft grass is something apparently belonging only to the New World.
- Socks - warm and woollen.
- Gloves - indispensable.

If you are travelling throughout Europe in summer you can always dispense with the pullover and other bulky items, and wear shorts and a T-shirt instead.

Health

Fitness

It is hopeless to set off on this holiday without being in some sort of reasonable physical shape. It is a good idea to have a regular routine of physical exercise.

If you are going to be doing a lot of walking, and you should be, then before you go, walk every day or every second day for an hour or so, and do some other exercises that take care of the muscles in the back and the arms. Practice lifting by bending your knees, strengthening the muscles around your thighs, as you may have to cart your luggage for uncomfortable distances across arduous uphill terrain. Decide thoroughly what you must take and what are optional extras. Calculate the weight you will be carrying and remember: "If in doubt leave out". Younger travellers may find this a little amusing, but it is amazing how many 20 year olds suddenly find that they are out of shape and worse off than the oldies, believing that natural physique and youth will get them through. No matter what your age, if you do not do regular sport, start engaging in some regular exercise so you can develop the stamina to stay enthusiastic for the duration of your trip.

Adjusting

As far as some travellers are concerned, a trip to Great Britain is an endurance-test just to get there. Hours and hours in a plane is no fun, especially if you are not travelling business or first class. Even then, it is still something of an ordeal: change of time zones, disruption of sleeping patterns, and your tour begins the very day you arrive! After two weeks you are shuffling back onto a plane, heading home while suffering the flu and other related ailments - and this was a holiday?

Normally the adrenaline is pumping, but as you are so tired after the long flight, you will tend to sleep well on the first night. If you arrive in the day, try to stay up until nightfall and go to bed at a similar time, if not a little earlier, than is the local custom. Then the next day you should be ready for action. Force your victimised system to adjust and run on British time. That way you can take advantage of the daylight hours. This is a holiday, so the stress of a normal working day routine is absent - be vibrant, energetic, and enjoy.

Medicine

Your medicine bag should include those medicines you may not only need to take, but also those you may need in unforseen situations. The idea is to be prepared.

• Paracetemol
• Tinea cream
• Antiseptic
• Needle
• Cotton
• Tissues
• Tweezers
• Something for an upset stomach (One aunt of the contributors recommends half a glass of brandy followed by half a glass of port wine to cure an upset stomach).
• Ear plugs, for both the plane and hotel. They are also handy if you want to go swimming.

Remember that the old inhalation method can help a fluey cold. All you need for this is a towel, boiling water and a basin. Some may wish to add eucalyptus oil. Then get a good night's sleep and maybe a day's rest if necessary.

On the Plane

Sleeping

Most airlines do not give **eye patches** to economy class passengers on long haul flights. Exceptions to this are Qantas and British Airways. So take them with you. Ask your travel agent for a pair or ask where can you purchase them. A $3 purchase will be well worth it. For sleeping on long flights, eye patches are essential, otherwise your journey will feel that much longer and whatever sleep you do get will be at best fitful.

Some people prefer to use medicinal drugs, but there are at least a couple of good reasons to avoid them and try to get some natural sleep instead. Though the trip may seem shorter because you are out of it for hours, what happens when two hours after takeoff the plane needs to divert to another destination because of a minor problem with an O ring in the starboard engine? In your sleeping-pill induced stupor you must now attempt to clamber off the plane. Then there are the very rare cases when an emergency occurs. At such times you want to be at your most alert, especially if you need to disembark quickly. And we have not even mentioned the possible side effects. So avoid pills if you can.

An extra pair of socks may come in handy. Over extended periods of inaction, when you are riveted to your seat, your feet are likely to become targets for the plane's air-conditioning and will feel the cold most acutely. You want to preserve them for all that walking you will be doing once you touch down in Great Britain. Also, on a 13 hour flight sector, it is amazing how comfort becomes critically important among a person's priorities of survival.

Alcohol

Alcohol does not really help either. The constant air-conditioning dehydrates the body and you end up with swollen feet - try putting your shoes back on if you have not moved your feet for hours. Beer can have you running backwards and forwards to the smallest room on the plane - so if you want to have a few drinks, do your fellow passengers a favour and get a seat on the aisle.

Where to Sit

Fortunately now most airlines have a no smoking policy throughout the aircraft for long haul flights. For most travellers this development was not too soon coming. The bronchia's tend to end up less clogged on a flight where smoking is not permitted than on those with a smoking section. Watch out for this on European-owned airlines such as Alitalia. Also, European airlines tend to overbook and you may be shuffled into the smoking section if there are problems with seat

Tower Bridge

allocation. Or you might end up in the smoking section because all the non-smoking seats are now occupied by a group of tourists on a package tour who booked four hours before you did. Since you only have a ruby frequent flyer card and not an emerald diamond, you will be ushered to the seat down the back next to the toilets. But you can't complain because you are lucky to have made the flight at all!

To try and avoid all this, it is best to have your seat allocated to you before you fly and make sure this is done for each leg or sector of your trip. If this cannot be achieved, try and check in early and see what the airline staff can do for you. It also helps to fly with an airline from your country of origin. They tend to realise that one benefit of accommodating you in Europe is that you might choose to fly with them domestically. After all, airlines developed frequent flyer programs precisely to give you that little extra perk which makes you feel important and persuades you to fly only with them. Use this marketing strategy to *your* advantage.

Give some consideration to where you prefer to be seated as it can contribute to being comfortable during the flight. Some people prefer to be seated in the back of the plane, others the front. The window is always the most popular. The emergency exit rows give you more leg room but you cannot spread out as the arms of the seats are fixed, whereas those in other rows can be moved up to increase your personal space. Also, in emergency exit rows luggage must be put in the overhead lockers, so you cannot have your carry-on luggage tucked into the pouch on the back of the seat in front of you for easy access. The aisle is fine as long as the person on the window or the middle does not get up too often during the flight. If you *are* stuck in the middle, politely ask the flight attendant if there is a chance you may be moved to either an aisle or a window seat. If not, console yourself with the thought that the flight will not last forever.

Airlines now advertise the pitch between the seats in economy class. Check these out, especially if you have long legs. This may determine your choice of airline, along with price, flight time to your destination, entertainment provided, and so on. Find out as much as you can about your intended airline and strive to tailor the flight to your needs.

Travel Agents

Booking on the web can be fine but certainly in the last couple of years travel agents have become much more professional - perhaps because they are competing with the web. Generally speaking they keep up-to-date by going on *famils* organised by airlines and travel wholesalers - the kinds of tour groups with whom you may end up. Some airlines see the agent as a vital link in their distribution channel. So when booking a flight or tour, the agent can put in a request for you; window seat, front of the plane, plenty of leg room, etc. An airline, if they can, will endeavour to accommodate the request. Agents can get good deals for you, sort out your wish list in half an hour and give you extra food for thought, whereas a convoluted web site may take a lot longer to navigate successfully. In addition, if you miss your flight they can put in a word for you and you may end up not having to pay a penalty fee. Remember that the web is closing in, but human contact remains alive and well.

Your Accommodation

It is important to set priorities based on your budget. Decide where you wish to splurge and give the credit card a work out at a luxurious four or five star hotel in the city centre, and where you will be content to stay in a comfortable, homely and relative inexpensive B&B on the outskirts of town.

The travel agent can book your accommodation for you. If you have no idea where to stay or the quality of accommodation that places offer, then get the travel agent to pursue this in detail for you. You can give your travel agent a budget and an idea of what sort of accommodation you want, what you expect from a hotel and where you want it to be located. A couple of extra dollars for a room will be more than compensated for by location, as you may not have to use public transport to reach the places you want to visit. Indeed, you will have more time for sightseeing if you are in the city centre.

This book gives you a range of hotels that vary in quality from excellent to ordinary, but all are clean and central. You can always go on the web and check out their prices there, or fax the hotel and ask for a quote, then compare this to what your agent can get for you. One thing about accommodation - try to get a room away from the street. Noise is a wonderful source of irritation for so many people.

It is a good idea to get the hotel reception to give you a wake up call - you're not here to sleep! Don't trust the alarm clock because both of you may be running on different time zones, and daylight saving may be a factor.

Web Addresses

To help familiarise yourself with Great Britain and Ireland before you visit, we have included web addresses of the main official national

Shopfront in Camden Town

tourism sites, plus a couple of others you may find useful, such as Eurail.

British Tourist Authority 👁www.bta.org.uk

Irish Tourist Board 👁www.itb.ie (👁www.ireland.travel.ie)

General Sites for Europe

Rail Pass Express 👁www.eurail.com

RailEurope 👁www.raileurope.com (info and commercial)

Europe Online 👁www.europeline.com

European Travel Commission 👁www.visiteurope.com

European Time Zones

A table for comparison, if you are coming in from another European city.

City	Hours from AEST	from GMT	from NY time
Amsterdam	-10	+1	+6
Athens	-9	+2	+7
Barcelona	-10	+1	+6
Berlin	-10	+1	+6
Brussels	-10	+1	+6
Copenhagen	-10	+1	+6
Dublin	-11	+0	+7
Frankfurt	-10	+1	+6
Lisbon	-11	0	+7
London	-11	0	+5
Madrid	-10	+1	+6
Manchester	-11	0	+5
Paris	-10	+1	+6
Rome	-10	+1	+6
Venice	-10	+1	+6
Vienna	-10	+1	+6
Zurich	-10	+1	+6

Clothing Sizes And Conversion Chart

Women's Clothing

Coats, Skirts, Dresses, Slacks, Jerseys, Pullovers

Aust/NZ	8	10	12	14	16	18
Europe	38	40	42	44	46	48
UK	8	10	12	14	16	18
USA	6	8	10	12	14	16

Shoes

Aust/NZ	4	5	$5^{1/2}$	6	$6^{1/2}$	7	$7^{1/2}$	8	$8^{1/2}$	9	$9^{1/2}$	10
Europe	34	36	37	37	38	38	39	40	40	41	41	-

UK	3	$3^{1/2}$	4	$4^{1/2}$	5	$5^{1/2}$	6	$6^{1/2}$	7	$7^{1/2}$	8	$8^{1/2}$
USA	$4^{1/2}$	5	$5^{1/2}$	6	$6^{1/2}$	7	$7^{1/2}$	8	$8^{1/2}$	9	$9^{1/2}$	10

Men's Clothing

Suits, Coats, Trousers, Jerseys, Pullovers

Aust/NZ	14	16	18	20	22	24
Europe	46	48	50	52	54	56
UK	36	38	40	42	44	46
USA	36	38	40	42	44	46

Shirts (Collar Sizes)

Aust/NZ	15	$15^{1/2}$	16	$16^{1/2}$	17	$17^{1/2}$
Europe (cm)	38	39	41	42	43	44
UK	15	$15^{1/2}$	16	$16^{1/2}$	17	$17^{1/2}$
USA	15	$15^{1/2}$	16	$16^{1/2}$	17	$17^{1/2}$

Shoes

Aust/NZ	8	9	10	11	12	13
Europe	42	43	44	46	47	48
UK	8	9	10	11	12	13
USA	$8^{1/2}$	$9^{1/2}$	$10^{1/2}$	$11^{1/2}$	$12^{1/2}$	$13^{1/2}$

Tipping

Generally speaking the cost of services involves a 10-15% tip to be added to the bill. Where a service charge is already imposed, there is no need to leave a tip unless the service is exceptional. With taxis in London one normally adds 10% to the fare.

Cameras and Film

For travellers to Great Britain and Ireland it is normally far cheaper to buy the film at your favourite camera shop duty free and have all the films processed when you return home. X-ray security machines in airports can damage photo film when it travels through them, if the film is exposed to this treatment too often on your trip. Better to keep the film roll tucked safely away in its little cylinder. One suggestion is to put all your film in a plastic bag and have it passed through the security check outside the machine.

Be sure to take spare batteries, since the duration of your trip and the fact that you can't remember when you last replaced them may mean a camera dies on you at the most inappropriate sightseeing time.

Mail and Contacting Home

The best way these days to let everyone at home now how your trip is progressing is to get an email address on a free email service such as Yahoo or Hotmail. Teach those in your family who don't know how to access emails before you leave. Addresses can be accessed in any cyber cafe - and there are plenty in Great Britain and Ireland. Or you may be staying with family or friends who are hooked up to the web.

Phone cards are an alternative that allow you to cap the cost of your calls and control your expenditures. VISA has a system which utilises access through a phone company and all you need is to find a public phone.

You can send mail care of an American Express office as long as the recipient has an AMEX card. You should check if they accept parcels. American Express offices will hold the mail for 30 days and this service is free. For most post offices the service is free also, though there may be a holding fee of a couple of dollars in some countries. If you are sending material or having it sent make sure the sender puts a return address on the letter or parcel.

Post offices also have the same system the world over. Just include as much information as possible on the parcel/package/postcard that your are sending.

Keeping Up-To-Date

Please note that because some places close and others open quite frequently, we would greatly appreciate hearing about it. Travel information must always be updated, developed and improved, so if over time any facts in this book have become incorrect, please let us know about it to help make your next Short Stay Guide accurate.

Have a great trip. We hope our guide enhances your Great Britain and Ireland experience.

Palace Guard

PART TWO

Great Britain

THE COUNTRIES THAT MAKE UP the United Kingdom, also called Great Britain, are England, Scotland, Wales and Northern Ireland. They cover an area of 244,100 sq km and have a total population of 58,123,000.

Not much is known about the history of England before the invasion by Julius Caesar, in 55BC, which made it a Roman province. The last Roman legions were withdrawn in 442AD leaving behind many temples, baths, forums, walls and paved highways that can still be seen today.

Peace was short-lived. The warring Picts and Scots from the north continually invaded, as did the Welsh from the west.

King Edward I of England subdued the Welsh and his son, the first Prince of Wales, was born at Caernarvon in 1284. This did not quell the rebellions but Henry VIII finally joined the two countries under the same system of laws and government.

The Romans tried unsuccessfully to capture Scotland but finally gave up and built a wall across the north of England. Scotland became united with England in 1603 when Mary Queen of Scots' son, James VI of Scotland became James I of England.

England, Scotland and Wales became united in 1707 under Queen Anne to form Great Britain.

Religious disputes have plagued Ireland since its beginning. Northern Ireland is largely Protestant, as a result of English migration. The rebellion of 1641 lasted eight years and paved the way for Oliver Cromwell to decimate the entire island, which had been ruled from London in oppressive fashion. In 1916 Sin Fein declared southern Ireland an independent state. After an impossible conflict for the British, Britain withdrew her troops and in 1921 the Irish Free State was proclaimed. Later the south became the Republic of Ireland and the north remained under British rule with a guaranteed protestant majority in political life.

Latest available population figures are: England 46,382,050, Scotland 4,962,152, Wales 2,811,865. English is spoken throughout the United

Kingdom. However, Gaelic is also spoken in some parts of Scotland. The Welsh also maintain their ancient Celtic tongue.

Climate

On the whole Britain has a cool climate. January is the coldest month with temperatures of 4C (39F). July and August are the warmest 16C (60F). The highest rainfall is in November with 97 mm. September is considered by many to be the best time of the year to visit. The temperature is 57F (14C), rainfall 3.2 ins (83 mm); there are less tourists to compete with; and prices fall. Tourist attractions and some hotels close at the end of September until Easter. April and May are also good months to visit. The spring flowers are in bloom and the temperature is reasonable.

Entry Regulations

All visitors must produce a valid passport. Commonwealth visitors staying less than six months do not require a visa. No vaccinations are required. The duty free allowance is 200 cigarettes or 100 cigarillos or 50 cigars or 250gm tobacco. Alcoholic drinks: 2 litres of still wine plus 1 litre of drinks over 22% vol, or 2 litres of alcoholic drinks under 22% vol or a further 2 litres of still wine. 60cc perfume, 250cc of toilet water. Other goods worth £145.

Currency

The currency of the land is the British Pound (£), which is divided into 100 pence. Approximate exchange rates, which should be used as a guide only, are:

A$	=	0.36£
Can$	=	0.48£
NZ$	=	0.31£
S$	=	0.40£
US$	=	0.66£

Notes are in denominations of £50, £20, £10, £5, andcoins are £2 £1, 50p, 20p, 10p, 5p, 2p and 1p. Scotland has its own notes and although English pounds are accepted in Scotland, you must change your Scottish pounds before you leave that part of the country. They are the same value and denomination as the English.

Major credit cards are widely accepted, but not by some leading stores (eg Marks & Spencer, John Lewis). You can obtain money from certain banks with your card. Check before leaving home as to which bank takes your card.

Changing travellers cheques can be expensive. There is a £4 commission charge at most banks and money exchanges. American Express travellers cheques can be changed free of commission at Lloyds and the Bank of Scotland. Thomas Cooks cheques at Thomas Cook outlets.

Banks are ☺open Mon-Fri 9.30am-4.30pm (Northern Ireland 10am-3.30pm). Some major banks open on Saturdays and for a few hours on Sundays, but all are closed on Public Holidays. Some banks in Scotland and Northern Ireland close for an hour at lunchtime.

Post offices are ☺open Mon-Fri 9am-5.30pm, and the main ones on Sat 9am-1pm (Northern Island until 12.30pm).

If you don't have a mailing address in the UK, it is best to have your mail sent to Poste Restante, Trafalgar Square Branch, 24-28 William IV Street, London WC2N 4DL. They will hold your mail for four weeks, and you must show proof of identity to collect it.

Most *shops* ☺open at 9.30am and close at 5.30pm, Mon-Sat. Small shops usually open at 9am. Late night shopping is Thursday when shops stay open until 8pm. Harrods opens at 10am and closes at 7pm. In suburbs many shops close for a half day on Wednesday or Thursday. In the country they often close for lunch.

Tax

VAT (value added tax) of 17.5% is charged on most goods and services. Non-EC residents may reclaim VAT but it has to be arranged through shops. Not all retailers participate and the value of the item is also considered. The goods must be shown to customs at your port of exit from Europe along with a form which the store will have given you. Shops usually charge a fee for the service. In other words, unless you have done some very expensive shopping it is not worth the trouble.

Telephone

It will cost more to phone from your hotel, so go to a pay phone. As a considerable amount of small change is needed to make even a local call, it is better to buy a phonecard. These are available from any British Tourist Information Centre, post offices and shops displaying the green phonecard sign. They come in £2, £5, £10 and £20 credit. For Overseas calls dial ©010 then the country code, the area code, then the number. Check the time difference in the phone book.

Driving

Driving is on the left-hand side of the road. The wearing of seat belts is compulsory. There are strong penalties for driving while under the influence of alcohol. Take your driving licence with you. People from certain countries only require their current licence. They can drive on it for one year. Countries not exempt need an International Driving Permit obtainable in your home town. Check before you leave home.

Road signs are almost all international. A copy of the highway code is obtainable from the AA, RAC, airports and car rental firms. The speed limits are as follows.

built up areas	-	30mph (48kph)
suburban areas	-	40mph (64kph)
motorways	-	70mph (113kph)
other roads	-	60mph (97kph)

Parking can be a headache. It is not allowed where there is an unbroken yellow line. Broken yellow or red lines indicate no stopping. As there are few parking meters, it is safer to go into a parking area where you put your money in a machine. If you park illegally, the authorities will clamp your wheels and you will have to pay a hefty fine - and suffer twenty-four hours of inconvenience!

Miscellaneous

Local time is GMT. Daylight saving operates from late March to late September.

Electricity is 240v AC. Take an adaptor or converter with you as the plugs are a different shape to those in other countries.

Health - Take any medication you require with you. It is also advisable to photocopy your prescriptions. Ask your doctor to give you a letter listing all medications you are on and any ailment from which you may suffer. Keep all medication in your overnight bag. It is essential to be covered for health insurance. It is also advisable to carry full insurance in case of emergencies.

Disabled facilities - Britain caters for the disabled. Most hotels and B&Bs have walk-in showers and ground floor rooms. British Rail and London Underground assist passengers on and off trains. With British Rail you must notify them the day before you travel. In the Underground simply ask one of the staff for assistance. Advice can be obtained from Holiday Care Service, 2 Old Bank Chambers, Station Road, Horley, Surry, ✆(0293) 774 535. Ask the British Tourist Authority for a Holiday Care enquiry form.

Pubs

Drinking hours in England and Wales are ☉11am-11pm weekdays, Sun midday-10.30pm; in Northern Ireland, Mon-Sat 11.30am-11pm, Sun 12.30pm-10pm; in Scotland, Mon-Sat 11am-11pm, Sun 12.30-2.30pm and 6.30-11pm.

All pubs serve food ranging from sandwiches and snacks to full hot dinners. There is no VAT on pub food which is usually of excellent quality.

Restaurants usually have a menu outside with the prices, and it is advisable to check this before entering or you could be in for a nasty shock. Remember to add the VAT and, in most cases, there is also a service charge.

Tipping

If a hotel or restaurant adds a service charge to your bill, there is no need to tip. Taxi drivers expect 10%, porters 50p a bag. Tipping is not so popular as in the past and is more confined to those who give extra service.

London

London is a huge metropolis with a permanent population of about 7,000,000 plus a floating population of workers and tourists. It really has something for everyone.

History

The oldest part in the city of London is a small square-mile patch, that was the original Roman Londinium. Although it is now the banking and commercial sector it also has some of the main tourist attractions. The City of Westminster is also another sector where many attractions can be found. Next there is the West End where the theatres and shops are located, and away from these main areas there is London, stretching out in all directions.

The Romans built their city at the highest point of the Thames, on Cornhills and Ludgate Hill. It was sacked by Bodicea in AD 61, and later attacked by the Vikings.

William the Conqueror built the White Tower of the Tower of London in the 11th century. The church and the 'guilds' sponsored building during the Middle Ages - St Bartholomew the Great 1123, St John of Jerusalem, Clerkenwell 1150, Temple Church 1185. Westminster Abbey was commenced in the 11th century. Southwick Cathedral, Westminster Hall, Lambeth Palace and the Guildhall were all built during this century.

By the 16th century, London had started to expand and St James Palace was erected. Queens House, Greenwich 1619-35. Banqueting Hall, Whitehall 1619-22, which has ceilings painted by Rubens. St Pauls Cathedral was built in 1665 and destroyed by fire in 1666. The Cathedral was replaced by Wren.

The 17th and 18th century saw more expansion with numerous squares designed by the Adams Brothers. These included Adelphi, Strand and Portland Place.

London was badly bombed during World War II but the damage has been repaired, with some historical buildings having been replaced by modern office blocks.

Tourist Information

British Tourist Authority has its head office at 1 Lower Regent Street. You can make reservations for transport, accommodation and theatre; change money, buy phonecards or shop for souvenirs. BTA information centres are located at all major railway stations.

Local Transport

You can go almost anywhere on the Underground, and easy to read maps show which route to take. Buses are frequent but because of the traffic, are not as fast. There are also Green Line buses to places outside the metropolitan area. Trains go in every direction. **Visitor Travelcards** are available for travel on the Underground and bus networks. They are available in 2, 3, 4 and 7-day formats, and must be purchased before you leave home. Available in the UK are: **One Day**

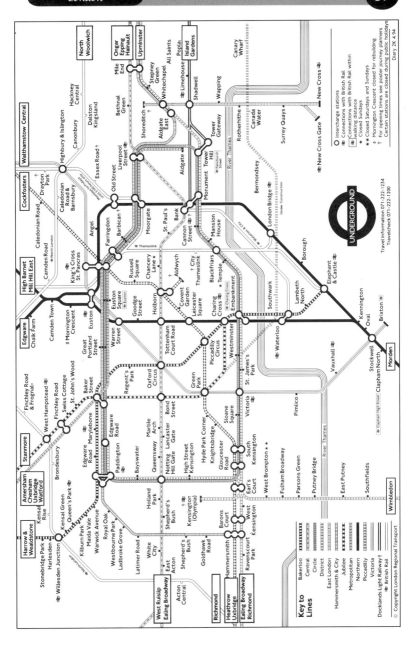

Key to Lines

Bakerloo
Central
Circle
District
East London
Jubilee
Metropolitan
Northern
Piccadilly
Victoria
Docklands Light Railway †
≠ British Rail

© Copyright London Regional Transport

UNDERGROUND

Travel Information 071-222-1234
Travelcheck 071-222-1200

Diary 2K 4.94

○ Interchange stations
≠ Connections with British Rail
⊞ Connections with British Rail within walking distance
* Closed Sundays
** Closed Saturdays and Sundays
◊ For opening times see poster journey planners
† Mornington Crescent closed for rebuilding
Certain stations are closed during public holidays

Travelcards (valid after 9.30am) which cost - ✪2 zones £3.80; 4 zones £4; all 6 zones £6.70 (children £1.90 all types); **Weekend Travelcards** (Sat and Sun) cost - ✪2 zones £5.70, 4 zones £6, zones 2-6 £4.90, all 6 zones £6.70 (children £2.80 all types) - a 25% saving on two one-day cards.

Family Travelcards are also available and can be used by any group of two adults and between one and four children travelling together, irrespective of whether they are related or not.

The *Carnet* pack buys 10 single tickets for zone 1 only and costs ✪£10 (a saving of £4).

For long term visitors there are weekly and monthly *Travelcards*. These can be obtained at Underground stations, but a passport size photograph is required.

Taxis are plentiful, and can be hired in the street, but a journey of a few miles within the central area will probably cost around ✪£6 (plus a 10% tip).

One of the best ways for a visitor to see London is by taking **The Original London Sightseeing Tour**. This is a hop-on/hop-off tour in an open-topped double decker bus that has 90 stops, and offers a choice between a live guided tour in English, or recorded commentaries that are available in a wide choice of languages. Open-dated vouchers can be purchased before arriving in the UK and costs are ✪£12.50 adult, £7.50 child 5-15.

Accommodation

Following is a selection of accommodation with prices for a double room per night, which should be used as a guide only.

Ritz, Piccadilly W1V 9D6, ✆(0171) 493-8181, fax(071) 493-2687 (✉travelweb@hotelbook.com(00702). 129 rooms. Stately, luxury hotel (noted for afternoon tea) decorated in the French style. Restaurant, bars, romantic Italian al fresco dining room. Handy distance to everything, transport at the door - ✪£290-385.

Sheraton Park Tower, 101 Knightsbridge, London, SW1X 7RN, ✆(171) 235 8050, fax 235 8231. A deluxe hotel situated in the heart of London with all the facilities expected of a 5-star hotel. For those who want to splurge. Three classes of accommodation - Classic ✪£221-280, Executive £264-380, Butler £660-1450.

Hotel Inter-Continental, 1 Hamilton Place, Hyde Park, London, W1V 0QY, ✆(0171) 409 3131, fax 493 3476. 460 room, bars, restaurants, everything the discerning traveller can possible need - ✪£195-330.

Amsterdam Hotel, 7 Trebovir Road, Earl's Court, London, SW5 9LS, ✆(0207) 370 5084, fax 244 7408 (✉reservations@amsterdam-hotel.com). Centrally located hotel with bar, restaurant and usual facilities. 27 rooms - ✪£80-160.

Comfort Inn Kings Cross, 2-5 Chad's Street, London, WC1H 8BD, ✆(0207) 837 1940, fax 278 5033. Centrally located with all amenities, plus continental breakfast - ✪£71-120.

Park Lodge Hotel

73 Queensborough Terrace, Bayswater, London, W2 3SU, ✆(0171) 229 6424, fax 221 4772 (✉travelweb@hotelbook.com(27512)). A peaceful residential terrace with 29 rooms situated close to Hyde Park - ✪£45-85.

Best Western Phoenix Hotel, 1-8 Kensington Gardens Square, London, ✆(0207) 229 2494, fax 727 1419. 125 rooms. A 3-star hotel within walking distance of Hyde Park, Oxford Street and city centre - ✪£63-86.

Stuart Hotel, 110-112 Cromwell Road, Kensington, London, SW7 4ES, ✆(0171) 373 1004, fax 370 2548 (✉travelweb@hotelbook.com(17032)). A tourist hotel with 50 rooms. A short walk from

Albert Hall and Gloucester Road Underground makes it a good base for sightseeing.

Lime Grove Hotel, 32 Lime Grove, Hammersmith, W12 8EA, ℂ(01817) 435 243, fax 400 364. A town house hotel with 15 rooms located 2 miles from Earl's Court. Cold buffet breakfast provided - ✪£48-75.

Food and Drink

Think of dining out in London and you will probably think of fish and chips, or bangers and mash, washed down with a pint of ale. These are still available, of course, but every other type of food you can imagine can also be found in London.

Beware of restaurants, though, with well-known names such as the ***Savoy***, ***Suntory***, or the ***Ivy***. They are all excruciatingly expensive, so it is best to investigate the menu outside before you enter. For best value go to the pubs, or British Home Stores and Littlewoods have cafeterias at reasonable prices.

Sightseeing

Among the main sights in the **City of London** is **St Paul's Cathedral**, which was designed by Sir Christopher Wren after the Great Fire of London destroyed its predecessor in 1666. Attractions in the Cathedral include the *Whispering Gallery*, the *Stone Gallery*, and the *Golden Gallery*, which offers superb views over London, and the tombs of the famous in the crypt. Take the underground to St Paul's Station. ☻Open Mon-Sat 8.30am-4pm; Galleries 9.30am-4pm, admission to the Cathedral and crypt is ✪£4 adult, £2 child; to galleries £3.50 adult, £1.50 child. Guided tours are available and cost £10 per person, which includes admission fees. For more information contact ℂ(0171) 246 8348 (✉stpauls.london.anglican.org).

The **Old Bailey**, built on the site of the infamous **Newgate Prison** is where most of the famous British criminals have been brought to justice. Seats in the public galleries are very much sort after so be early. Close to the Old Bailey is the **"Old Lady of Threadneedle Street"**, more formally known as the Bank of England. In this vicinity you can see the lane where the fire of London started; visit pubs frequented by Bacon, Dickens and many more; but the most impressive building in the city is the **Tower of London**.

The *White Tower* was built in the time of William the Conqueror. The *Bloody Tower* is where the young Princes were murdered by King Richard III. *Traitor's Gate* lives up to its murky reputation, and visitors can gaze on the spot where Ann Boleyn and Catherine Howard kept their appointments with the executioner. On the brighter side you can see the crown jewels displayed in well illuminated glass cases. The Underground is the quickest way to the Tower - use Tower Station. ☉Open Mon-Sat 9am-5pm, Sun 10am-5pm, and admission is ✪£10.50 adult, £6.90 child, ✆(0171) 709 0765 (☞www.hrp.org.uk).

By contrast, the **City of Westminster** has wide streets with lots of parklands. Here are found the **Houses of Parliament**, and the spot where Charles I was condemned to death in the **Palace of Westminster** next door (use Westminster Station).

Westminster Abbey stands across the road. Here all the kings and queens except Edward V and Edward VIII have been crowned. Many famous royals, statesmen and poets have been buried here (use St James Station). ☉Open Mon-Sat with last admissions 3.45pm Mon-Fri, 1.45pm Sat. Admission is £5 adult, £2 child, ✆(0171) 222 5152 (☞www.westminster-abbey.org). Guided Tours are available, and are well-worth taking - ✪£3 per person, ✆(0171) 222 7110.

Stroll up **Northumberland Avenue**, past the many offices that house the Admiralty, War Office and Foreign Office, to the **Cenotaph** and then into **Downing Street** where the Prime Minister lives. In the last street on the right, just before **Trafalgar Square** there is a pub called the *Sherlock Holmes* which serves excellent meals. It also has a museum of Sherlock Homes memorabilia.

Once in Trafalgar Square you will see the tall column with **Lord Nelson** on the top. **St Martin's-in-the-Fields** church, the **National Gallery** and the **Reference Library** are all in this vicinity. Passing through the **Admiralty Arch** leads to **The Mall** with **Buckingham**

Palace at the end. The palace's state rooms are open seven days a week to tourists when the Queen is away on her summer break, usually from early August to late September or early October. Admission prices are high, and there are always long queues, but it is still worth a visit. Tickets can be purchased at the booth in the park opposite, or ✆(0171) 321 2233 and use a credit card. The **Changing of the Guard** is held at ⏰11.30am every day in summer and every second day in winter. In order to get a good view it is imperative to get there at least an hour before it starts, but again, the wait is worth it. For more information, ✆(0171) 414 2353.

Those interested in World War II, should visit the **Cabinet War Rooms**, Clive Steps, King Charles Street, ✆(0171) 930 6961 (👁www.iwm.org.uk). This is where Winston Churchill and his advisors made their decisions and planned their strategies. There are 21 underground rooms presented as they were in the 1940s (use Westminster Station). ⏰Open 10am-6pm, admission ✪£4.80 adult, children free.

Take the Underground to Baker Street, turn into Marylebone Road and visit **Madame Tussaud's Waxworks**, ✆(0171) 935 6861, and **London Planetarium**, ✆(0171) 486 1121. Both establishments are usually ⏰open Mon-Fri 10am-5.30pm, Sat-Sun 9.30am-5.30pm, but it is best to ring and confirm. Admission to the waxworks is ✪£10.50 adult, £7 child, and to the Planetarium, £6 adult, £4 child, but there are combined tickets available for £12.25 adult, £8.50 child.

Madame Tussaud's is one of those places that you can visit every time you are in the neighbourhood, because new 'people' are always being displayed, or old 'people' are returning after a bit of rejuvenation. In the Planetarium audiences can embark on a journey through time, or watch the feature *Planetary Quest* which lasts for 40 minutes and shows ☉daily from 9.30am during school holidays and from 12.20pm at other times, with the last show commencing 5pm.

Museums
The British Museum and British Library, Great Russell Street, ©(0171) 636 1555 (☞www.british-museum.ac.uk). Take the Underground to Tottenham Court Road or Russell Square. ☉Open Mon-Sat 10am-5pm, Sun noon-6pm, and there is no admission fee, but guided tours are available from ✪£5-7. This is the world's oldest museum (1753) and one of its most fascinating. There are 2.5 miles of galleries with artefacts from almost every aspect of international cultural history. Anyone interested in Egyptology could spend a week in this museum. There is the Rosetta Stone; the recent addition of Roxie Walker Galleries of Egyptian Funerary Archaeology presenting an unparalleled collection of mummies; and dear old *Ginger*, a predynastic man who died pre-3100BC, befores the practice of mummification, but is here in all his glory.

Dickens House Museum, 48 Doughty Street, ©(0171) 405 2127 (☞www.rmplc.co.uk/orgs/dickens). Although Charles Dickens and his family only lived here for two years or more (1837-1839), it was during that time that he wrote *The Pickwick Papers*, *Oliver Twist* and *Nicholas Nickleby*, and made his name in English literature. The house has probably the most comprehensive Dickens library in the world, and is ☉open Mon-Sat 10am-5pm. Admission is ✪£4 adult, £2 child (Russell Square Station).

The Museum of London, London Wall, ✆(0171) 600 3699 (👁www.museumoflondon.org.uk) traces the growth of the city from prehistoric times to the present day (use St Paul's Station). ☉Open Mon-Sat 10am-5.50pm, Sun noon-5.50pm. Admission is ✪£5 adult, children free.

Victoria and Albert Museum, Cromwell Road, ✆(0171) 938 8500 (👁www.vam.ac.uk) is ☉open daily 10am-5.45pm and admission is £5 adult, child under 18 free (4.30-5.45pm admission free). This is a museum of decorative arts, with 146 galleries exhibiting: a collection of over 400 years of European fashion; the Raphael Gallery; the Silver Galleries; and the Canon Photography Gallery. (Use South Kensington Station.)

Kensington Palace State Apartments, Kensington Gardens, ✆(0171) 937 9561 (👁www.hrp.org.uk). ☉Open Wed-Sun 10am-3pm, and admission is ✪£8.50 adult, £6.10 child. William III and Mary acquired the palace in 1689 as a country retreat, but it is better known now as the home of the late Diana, Princess of Wales. There are changing displays, but often they are of special occasion clothes worn by the present Royals. (Use Queensway or High Street Kensington Stations.)

Shakespeare's Globe Exhibition, New Globe Walk, Bankside, ✆(0171) 902 1500 (👁www.shakespeares-globe.org), is ☉open daily 10am-5pm, and admission is ✪£7.50 adult, £5 child (subject to change). While not strictly a museum, the exhibition features the story of the Globe Theatre, the *in* place in Shakespeare's day. All aspects of Elizabethan theatre are covered, including the roles of the playwright, the actor, the audience, and the architects and craftsmen who built the playhouses of that time. Not to be missed by fans of the Bard of Avon.

Walking in London

Walking allows the visitor to discover places that are not found on the 'tourist routes'. In almost every street there are houses with plaques that commemorate the famous people who lived there. Sundays are never dull in London. You can take the Underground to **Hampstead**, walk up the hill towards the heath and look at the pavement artists. Then have lunch at one of the famous pubs, for example *Jack Straws Castle* which was a favourite watering hole of Dick Turpin the Highwayman, or stroll across the heath to the *Spaniards*, also the haunt of highwaymen. The *Bull and Bush*, immortalized in song, has been rebuilt, and across the road is **Anna Pavlova's house** in Golders Hill Park where deer roam free. Museums, art galleries and many other attractions are all open on Sundays.

Covent Garden is at its liveliest at weekends, and singers and other artists entertain in front of **St Paul's Church**. This is known as the Actors' church and many memorials are found inside. The former wholesale fruit and vegetable market now has shops and a market which has some interesting goods at reasonable prices. The **London Transport Museum** and the **Theatre Museum** are both nearby, and just around the corner stands the **Royal Opera House** and **Drury Lane** theatre. Those who prefer horticulture can take the Underground to Kew and wander around **Kew Gardens**, ⏰open daily 9.30am-5pm, ✪£5 adult, £2.50 child, ✆(0181) 940 1171.

Sights Further Afield

It is possible to go by Green line bus, or train, to visit **Windsor Castle**, but the best way is to take a tour that includes a visit to nearby **Eton School** and **Runnymede**, where King John signed the Magna Carter in 1215. Windsor Castle is quite breathtaking when you first lay eyes on it, and in fact, it covers 13 acres. The Queen lives here for part of the year, usually Christmas, Easter and Ascot week, but even so some of the royal apartments are open to the public, as are the Round Tower, St George's Chapel, where Henry VIII and Charles I are buried, and the Royal Dolls House. Admission is ✪£10 adult, which is pretty steep, but remember they have to pay for the £80 million restoration work that followed the 1992 fire.

Hampton Court Palace, Surrey, ✆(0181) 781 9500 (👁www.hrp.org.uk) is a must-see. It is ⊙open Mon 10.15am-4.30pm, Tues-Sun 9.30am-4.30pm. Admission to State Apartments, Maze and Privy Garden is ✪£10 adult, £6.60 child; to the Maze only £2.30 adult, £1.50 child; to Privy Garden only £2.10 adult, £1.30 child. Cardinal Wolsey, Archbishop of York commenced building the palace in 1514, but later thought it prudent to make a gift of it to his sovereign, Henry VIII, who added the Chapel Royal's magnificent roof. Make sure you don't miss the tennis court, and incredibly old grapevine, and of course, try your luck with the Maze. Allow plenty of time here as there is plenty to see and do.

Canterbury and Woburn Abbey are also within easy reach of London.

The Best of London in Brief

Westminster Abbey. Built in 1065, the Abbey has been the site of every royal coronation save two since that of William the Conquerer in 1066. It contains the remains of 29 monarchs and houses 3,000 tombs. Highlights of a walk through this majestic building and through its 900 years of history include the shrine of Edward the Confessor, the Coronation Chair,

Henry VII Chapel, Poet's Corner, the Tomb of Queen Elizabeth I and Mary I, and the Nave. Although crowds are always heavy, this is without question one of Great Britain's premier attractions. *Broad Sanctuary*.

Tower of London. Bursting at the seams with visitors, this historical fortress is well-worth a wait in the queues. The White Tower with its thick walls was built by William the Conquerer in the twelfth century, not only for defence but also as a signature of strength. While torture certainly took place here, it was not quite the order of the day. Plenty of heads belonging to famous traitors, wives whose husbands grew tired of them, or stoic Catholics, made their way onto the cold stone floor without a shoulder to lean on. The Crown Jewels, of which St. Edward's Crown is the oldest piece (1061) and the Sovereign's Scepter bears a 530-carat diamond, are kept here. Other highlights of the fortress include the Bloody Tower where prisoners were kept, the Medieval Palace and the picturesque Tower Bridge. *Tower Hill*.

British Museum. The best insight into the history of civilisation, from the ancient worlds of Egypt, Greece, Assyria Asia, Mexico and Africa to modern worlds. Highlights include the Rosetta Stone, part of a huge statue of Ramses II, Egyptian mummies, the Elgin Marbles, the Sutton Hoo Anglo-Saxon burial ship and countless other scultpures and relics. *Great Russel Street*.

Buckingham Palace. This colossal residence is always high on the itinerary of visitors to London, particularly on days when the Changing of the Guard ceremony is scheduled. *The Mall*.

St. Paul's Cathedral. England's national church took 35 years to build. This architectural masterpiece was completed in 1710. Its main dome rises 365-feet into the air and is the world's second largest. Wellington, Nelson, Nightingale and the church's designer, Sir Christopher Wren are among those laid to rest in the crypt. *St Paul's Churchyard*.

Houses of Parliament. The Houses of Parliament are contained in the former residence of British royalty, the Palace of Westminster, which was largely destroyed in a fire in 1834 and rebuilt in Gothic Revival style. Both the House of Commons and House of Lords can be visited within when in session. Highlights inside are the Westminster Hall and Jewel Tower. The sight of this 1000-room building lining the bank of the Thames, with its clock tower containing the Big Ben bell soaring above, is the quintessential image of London. *Parliament Square*.

Cabinet War Rooms. The underground headquarters of the British government, as used by Churchill and his advisors during World War II, has been left in its 1945 state. *King Charles Street*.

National Gallery. Displaying Britain's best offering of European art from the thirteenth century to modern Impressionism, this great gallery has works by da Vinci, Botticelli, Michelangelo, Leonardo, Bruegel, Titian, van Gogh, Rembrandt, Monet, Cezanne, and many others, which are wonderfully explained in an audio tour. *Trafalgar Square*.

Victoria and Albert Museum. A gallery of Decorative Arts, with rooms devoted to English fashion, the work of Raphael and Donatello, medieval European art, legitimate copies of famous art and some notorious forgeries. *Cromwell Road*.

Harrods. Europe's most extravagent department store is in Knightsbridge. It has a staggering array of goods and an amazing food court that should be visited. Beware that it also has some of the most eye-popping price tags you will find. *87-135 Brompton Road*.

Trafalgar Square. Located in the centre of London, this famous square is a bustling hive of activity. Sit on the steps and take in your surrounds; the statue of Lord Nelson, the lions, the milling pedestrians and the many hungry pigeons.

Globe Theatre. Shakespeare fans should head to the master wordsmith's home ground, faithfully recreated to appear as it did in his day, which contains details of his life and work and also puts on performances. *Near Southwark Bridge*.

Tate Gallery of British Art. Covering five centuries of British art, the highlights of the gallery are pieces by Turner, Blake, Gainsborough and Hogarth. *Millbank*.

Tate Gallery of Modern Art. This terrific museum features the twentieth century works of Picasso, Warhol, Monet and their contemporaries. *Near Globe Theatre*.

Piccadilly Circus. Like Trafalgar Square, Piccadilly is brimming with people, the difference being that most of them here are tourists. Segaworld, an IMAX theatre and Chinatown are attractions in the area.

National Portrait Gallery. Famous British faces are captured here on canvas, from Henry VIII to Shakespeare to Princess Diana. *St. Martin's Place*.

Covent Garden. Overrated shopping precinct that has the interesting London Transport Museum nearby.

Hyde Park. Covering more than 600 acres, famous Hyde Park, once the hunting grounds of Henry VIII, contain Speakers' Corner, Serpentine Lake, comfortable benches and plenty of grass.

British Library. An invaluable collection of old maps, Bibles, the original Magna Carta, manuscripts from early English literature including Shakespeare's folios, and selections of important music lyrics. *96 Euston Road.*

Natural History Museum. A fascinating look at the two worlds of biology and geology, covering the human body and evolution, and our planet's development and natural disasters. *Cromwell Road.*

Madame Tussaud's Waxworks. A famous gallery of well-known wax bodies with their well-known wax heads. *Marylebone Road.*

Apsley House. The displays in the Wellington Museum were collected by the Duke of Wellington, who defeated Napolean at Waterloo, and include artworks by Velazquez and Canova. *149 Piccadilly, Hyde Park Corner.*

Museum of London. If you are interested in the history of the city, stretching back before the days of Roman occupation, this capable museum will quench your thirst. *150 London Wall.*

Millennium Bridge. A new sleek pedestrian bridge crossing the Thames.

British Airways London Eye. An enormous Ferris wheel providing the highest possible viewpoint in the city without the aid of an aircraft.

Kenwood House. Its stunning interior is enhanced by an art collection including works by Rembrant and Gainsborough. *Hampstead Lane*.

Imperial War Museum. Covers warfare of the last century in great detail, offering insights into the monumental events that wracked the world and defined the tumultuous history of the 1900s. *Lambeth Road*.

York

North-west of London is the walled city of York with a population of around 100,000. Cars are not permitted inside the city walls.

York was founded by the Romans in 71AD and its Roman name was Eboracum, however Viking remains have been excavated and are now on show in the Jorvik Viking museum.

Tourist Information

British Tourist Authority have an office at the railway station and another in Tower Street, City centre.

The Yorkshire Tourist Board is at 312 Tadcaster Road, York, ✆(01904) 707 070, fax 701 414 (👁www.ytb.org.uk).

Local Transport

The best way to see the sights is to take the Sightseeing Bus, which you can get off and on as often as you like.

Accommodation

The Parsonage Country House Hotel Escrick, York, ✆(01904) 728 111, fax 728 151. Close to all major link roads, but only 10 minutes from the centre of York. 22 cosy rooms with ensuites - ✪£66-80 per person.

The Grange Hotel, 1 Clifton, York, ℂ(01904) 644 744, fax 612 453 (✉info@grangehotel.co.uk), 5 minutes from the Minster and city walls. 30 rooms with en-suites, licensed, 3 restaurants - ✪£50-66 per person.

Midway House Hotel, 145 Fulford Road, York, ℂ/fax (01904) 659 272. Located on A19 south of city centre. 12 en-suite bedrooms, full English breakfast, no smoking - ✪£36-50 per person.

Self Catering

Abbey House Self Catering Apartments, 7 St Mary's, York, ℂ(01904) 636 154, fax 612 340. Situated in the heart of York. 20 units sleeping 1-6, bed linen, towels, heating, colour TV - ✪£125-385 per unit per week.

Cloisters Walk, 1 St Mary's, York, ℂ(01904) 638 915. Close to the Minster. 2 units sleeping 2-4. Well equipped, electricity and linen included, no smoking - £200-340.

The Wasps Nest Holiday Cottages, Green Hammerton, York, ℂ(01423) 330 153, fax 331 204. Central for exploring the Dales and moors, towns, abbeys and stately homes. 4 units sleeping 1-5, owner supervised - ✪£150-390 per unit per week.

Food and Drink

You cannot really claim to have been to York unless you have sampled Yorkshire pudding, made as only the locals can. The batter is formed into a deep circle with a base and filled with cooked beef and onion gravy.

There are plenty of cafes and other eating houses that serve reasonably priced food. Most restaurants serve good wholesome English food. Tea houses are popular.

Sightseeing

The **Gothic Minster** is the most famous building in York. It has an 11 tonne bell, known as Big Peter, which tolls every day at noon.

Take the time to look at the soaring columns, the choir screen portraying the kings of England and the rose window which commemorates the marriage of King Henry VII to Elizabeth of York.

Visit the Chapter House built in the 13th century.

The narrow streets of York are full of surprises and are well worth wandering through. **Clifford's Tower** stands perched on a grassy mound. Museums abound: **York Castle**, **National Railway**, **Friargate**, **Regimental**, **Bar Convent**, **Museum of Automata** and the **York Dungeon**, an animated horror museum.

You can walk along the 13th century walls, and look at the medieval half wooden shops and houses in the centre of the city called the **Shambles**.

York also has the most fashionable shopping centre in the north of England.

Sights Further Afield

Within easy reach, and well worth seeing, are **The Yorkshire Dales**. Apart from the beauty of the scenery, this is James Herriott (*All Creatures Great and Small*) country. You will see where the real surgery was, the church where he was married and the locations for the TV show.

Another great tour is to **Castle Howard**. This was the stately home used in the TV series *Brideshead Revisited*. The castle was built between 1699 and 1759, and the state rooms are lavish, the chapel interesting and the costume museum well worth seeing. The grounds are beautiful and time should be made to wander through them. The house is occupied by the Howard family.

Yet another interesting tour is to Bronte Country and **Emmerdale**. On this tour you can watch traditional clogs being made.

It will be easy to understand how the countryside inspired Emily Bronte to write *Wuthering Heights*.

The Best of York in Brief

York Minster. Built on an historic site which once bore a Roman fort, then a Norman church and now this huge Gothic cathderal, York Minster has great views from its Central Tower and provides interesting details of its construction in the Foundations Museum. Its magnificent interior is replete with Gothic and Romanesque art and architecture. This is one of York's top attractions. *Deangate*.

York Castle Museum. A terrific museum, one of Europe's best, with a recreation of the streets and shops of old York, World War II memorabilia, a lively history of household appliances and much more. *The Eye of York*.

National Railway Museum. A comprehensive look at 150 years of rail history in a world-class museum. Photographs, interactive exhibitions, wonderful models and displays make this a fascinating experience. *Leeman Road*.

Merchant Adventurers' Hall. This old Guild Hall is a national treasure with plenty of historical significance. First built in the fourteenth century and rebuilt in the fifteenth century, it contains the Great Hall where meetings and business were conducted, the Undercroft where charity and medical help were administered and the Chapel where prayers were taken. Even the wood, stone and bricks used as building materials are themselves significant. *Fossgate*.

Jorvik Viking City. Archaelogical evidence found on this site inspired the detailed recreation of Jorvik, a tenth century Viking city. Astonishing depth has gone into the production, designed to transport the visitor back to this age in every possible way. *Coppergate*.

City Walls. Part of York's medieval walls still stand and you can walk along them for fine views of the city while reflecting on the centuries they stood protecting it.

Yorkshire Museum. 1000 years of the city's heritage are captured here in a good collection of Roman, Viking, Anglo-Saxon, Norman and Gothic artifacts. *Museum Gardens*.

Yorkshire Air Museum. For those interested in wartime aircraft, the focus of this musuem is on World War II, with reconstructions of several planes, a Control Tower and a Squadron Room. These are accompanied by a detailed history of several wartime inventions. *Halifax Way Elvington*.

York Dungeon. Recounts York's bloody Viking past and Guy Fawkes' 'Gunpowder Plot'. *12 Clifford Street*.

The Shambles. A popular pedestrian street whose people and ambience attracts the tourists.

Castle Howard. Situated on over 1000 acres of natural and landscaped parkland, this beautiful palace was built in the eighteenth century and is the largest residence (still occupied by the Howard family) in Yorkshire.

The Lake District

The Lake District is a beautiful slice of England. The lakes are separated by rugged hills rising about 900m - high by English standards. The scenery is soft and has a soothing effect. It's no wonder it was home to so many poets and writers. To appreciate the area you really need to do a lot of walking.

William Wordsworth lived from 1799 to 1808 at Dove Cottage in the town of Grasmere. The cottage and an adjoining museum are open to the public (⋏ ww@dovecott.demon.co.uk). Wordsworth spent the last 17 years of his life at nearby Rydal Mount which is also open to the public. He died in 1850 and was buried in Grasmere churchyard where his grave can be seen.

Windermere is the largest lake in England and also the name of the tourist town that lies on its east bank. It is popular with yachtsmen and boaters. Regular trips around the lake are run by the Iron Steamboat Company.

Wast Water has the most spectacular mountains in the district but is not accessible by road. **Keswick** has the Fitz Park Museum which has manuscripts and letters written by some of the famous authors who lived and wrote some of their best known works while living in the area. Samuel Coleridge moved here in 1800 and lived at Greta Hall. Other writers whose work is displayed include Robert Southey and John Ruskin. Sir Hugh Walpole wrote his famous *Herries Saga* when living in the district. His works are also on display.

Hawkeshead has the building where Wordsworth went to school. It is open to the public. You can also see Ann Tyson's cottage where Wordsworth stayed when a schoolboy.

Sawrey is where Beatrix Potter lived in a country house at Hill Top. The house, with her original manuscripts and drawings, is open to the public from Easter to the end of October.

Tourist Information

Cumbria Tourist Board, Ashleigh, Holly Road, Windermere, ©(015394) 44 444, fax 44 041 (✆www.cumbria-the-lake-district.co .uk, ✎mail@cumbria-tourist-board.co.uk).

Accommodation

Following is a selection of accommodation with prices for a double room per night, which should be used as a guide only.

Gilpin Lodge Hotel

Crook Road, Windermere, ©(015394) 88 818, fax 88 058 (✎hotel@gilpin-lodge. co.uk). Situated 2 miles from Lake Windermere and 12 miles from M6. 14 rooms with en-suite, licensed, good restaurant - ✪£66-80.

Storrs Hall, Windermere, ©(015394) 47 111, fax 47 555. Georgian hall set on the shores of Lake Windermere. 4 rooms with en-suite, restaurant with great views - ✪£80+.

Low Wood Hotel, Windermere, ©(015394) 33 338, fax 34 072 (👁www.elh.co.uk, ✎lowwood@elh.co.uk). 117 rooms with en-suite situated on shore of Lake Windermere, 2 restaurants, 3 bars, watersport centre, leisure club - ✪£50-66.

The Fairfield, Bowness-on-Windermere, ©/fax (015394) 46 565 (✎ray&barb@the-fairfield.co.uk). 200 year-old-house close to village and lake. Licensed, leisure club, great hospitality - ✪£26-36.

Holly Lodge, 6 College Road, Windermere, ©/fax (015394) 43 873. 6 rooms with en-suite situated close to shops, restaurants and transport. Good English breakfast - ✪£16-26.

The Best of The Lake District in Brief

Derwentwater. This very picturesque lake is best for a leisurely sail on its waters or a stroll along its shores.

Keswick. This town rests against the north eastern part of Derwentwater and is the place where graphite was first discovered and the famous Derwent pencils are now made. There is a Pencil Museum in town which traces this history.

Buttermere. A relatively small but beautiful lake, Buttermere has a 6.5km perimeter which can be followed on an idyllic walk.

Castlerigg Stone Circle. One of those inexplicable sights that pops up in the United Kingdom, this one comprises stones that are over three millenniums old and which seem to have strange geometric links with the surrounding landscape.

Dove Cottage. This is the former residence of the famous English poet William Wordsworth, who occupied the country retreat while in his creative prime. It is a good way to see the environment in which he worked and gain an understanding of his appreciation for nature. There is a good little museum adjacent.

Beatrix Potter's Farm. Peter Rabbit and Jemima Puddleduck were among those famous creations who sprung to life in this seventeenth century cottage. The cluttered rooms contain original drawings and details of the author's life.

Hikes and Walks. The Lakes District takes in some of Britain's most attractive countryside. Walking or hiking is the best way to immerse yourself in it, and there are innumerable trails to tread.

Manchester

Manchester is situated on the River Irwell which is linked to the Mersey estuary by the Manchester ship canal, built in 1894. It is a main port and the second biggest commercial city in England with a population of around 450,000.

Probably the most famous things that Manchester has produced are the television series *Coronation Street*, and the champion soccer team, Manchester United.

History

Originally it was the Roman fort of Mancuniom, and during the mid-eighteenth century, it became the cotton capital of the world, although most of the cotton mills are outside the city. Today it is a thriving industrial centre producing chemicals, clothing, printed goods, publishing, paper, food products, rubber and electrical goods.

The airport is less congested than Heathrow and passengers can take the fast rail link and be in the city in 20 minutes. It is a good starting point for touring the various regional areas of Britain outside of London.

Machester claims to be the city where the first atom was split; the first passenger railway station was built; the first test-tube baby was born; the first public library was opened; the first British plane was flown; and the first commercial computer was developed. Quite an achievement for a place that was a village 200 years ago.

Tourist Information

British Tourist Authority has an office at the railway station.

The North West Tourist Board is at Swan House, Swan Meadow Road, Wigan Pier, Wigan, ℰ(01942) 821 222, fax 820 002 (✆www.visitbritain.com/north-west-england, email ✉info@nwrb.u-net.com)

Local Transport

There are buses and trains to wherever you wish to go. Manchester is not really a tourist city, so it does not have the usual infrastructure.

Accommodation

Following is a selection of accommodation with prices for a double room per night, which should be used as a guide only.

Crowne Plaza Manchester-The Midland, Peter Street, Manchester, ℰ(0161) 236 3333, fax 932 4100 (✆www.crowneplaza.co.uk). Set in the heart of the city close to theatres, Granada Studios, Old Trafford and shopping areas - 303 rooms with en-suite, restaurants, bars - ✪£80+.

Portland Thistle Hotel, 3-5 Portland Street, Piccadilly Gardens, Manchester, ℰ(0161) 228 3400, fax 228 6347. Located in the heart of the city. 205 rooms with en-suite, restaurants, bars - ✪£66-80.

The Princess Hotel, 101 Portland Street, Manchester, ©(0161) 236 5122, fax 236 4468. Situated in city centre close to shopping area and theatres. 85 rooms with ensuite, restaurant, bars - ✪£26-36.

Food and Drink

There are plenty of places to eat and drink in Manchester, but there are no special dishes that the city can call its own. Check the menus outside restaurants before entering.

Sightseeing

Although it has been transformed into a modern go-ahead city, many of Manchester's Victorian buildings have been restored.

Manchester Cathedral, built as a church in the 15th century, is well worth a visit.

Some of the best known features of this city are the *Guardian*, first published in 1821 as the Manchester Guardian; The Halle Orchestra; the Grammar School; the Institute of Science and Technology; and the University, all established in the 19th century. Cricket fans know Manchester from Test Matches played at **Old Trafford** and soccer fans either love or hate *Manchester United*.

The Best of Manchester in Brief

The Currier Gallery of Art. This great little museum has paintings, sculptures and decorative arts from America and Europe spanning the era from the Renaissance to modern times. Highlights are the pieces by Monet and Picasso. Tours can be taken through Zimmerman House, listed on the National Register of Historic Houses and designed by American architect Wright in 1950. *201 Myrtle Way*.

Pump House People's History Museum. Traces Manchester's social working culture and some of the highs and lows of its historical events. *Left Bank, Bridge Street*.

Manchester Cathedral. Noted for its wood carvings from the fifteenth century and the fact that it contains the country's widest nave. *Cathedral Yard*.

Manchester Historic Association. A library and museum detail the industrial history of this working town. They also provide maps for heritage walking tours past the city's eighteenth century buildings and distinct row houses. *129 Amherst St*.

The Museum of Science & Industry. This is a large museum occupying five buildings (actually a former passenger railway station - the oldest in the world) with a variety of exhibits that interpret the human body, the earth, space and much more. There are also changing seasonal programs. *Liverpool Road*.

Chester

The quaint, old city of Chester stands on the River Dee. Although it is the capital of the county of Cheshire, its population is only around 59,000.

History

In 70AD the Romans built a fortress called Deva where Chester now stands. They used it when they were endeavouring to conquer the north, and it was occupied by the 20th Legion for 300 years. Chester was the last town in England to yield to William the Conqueror in 1070, so he repaid the people of the area by confiscating their land. After the Norman conquest, Cheshire was made a palatine - province of a feudal lord - under the Earl of Chester. It had its own parliament but the Earl owned all the land except that belonging to the church. This situation remained the same until the reign of Henry VIII.

Cheshire is rich in literary traditions. Raphael Holinshed was the chief author of a history of Britain, on which Shakespeare based fourteen of his plays. Charles Lutwidge Dodgson, better known as Lewis Carroll, author of *Alice in Wonderland*, was born in a vicarage near Warrington. Elizabeth Gaskell immortalised the village of Knutsford in her book *Cranford*. William Congreve, the Restoration dramatist, also lived in the area. Religious figures linked with Chester include hymn writer Bishop Heber and missionary explorer Sir Wilfred Grenfell.

Tourist Information

The British Tourist Authority has an office at the station.

The Chester Visitor and Craft Centre is in Vicars Lane, Chester, ©(01244) 603 127, fax 602 2620 (✍ g.tattum@chestercc.gov.uk).

Local Transport

The best way to see Chester is on the Explorer bus. It is a double decker and can be boarded anywhere. Fares can be paid on the bus but you save ✪£1 if you buy it in advance from BTA.

Keep your ticket as this entitles you to another reduction if you take an explorer trip in another city.

Accommodation

Following are a couple of accommodation possibilities with prices for a double room per night, which should be used as a guide only.

The Grosvenor-Pulford Hotel, Wrexham Road, Pulford, ©(01244) 570 560, fax 570 809 (✪www.grosvenorpulfordhotel.co.uk, email ✍ grosvenor@btinternet.com). Situated 3 miles from the city of Chester in magnificent countryside. 70 rooms with en-suite, swimming pool, health club, restaurant, bar - ✪£36-50.

Forest Hills Hotel

Bellemonte Road, Overton Hill, Frodsham, ©(01928) 735 255, fax 735 517 (✎113002.1271@compuserve.com). Close to M56 in scenic countryside. 57 rooms with ensuite. Swimming pool, sauna, steam room, squash courts, restaurant, bar - ✪£36-50.

Food and Drink

There are plenty of restaurants, tea shops and pubs where you can have a good English meal.

Sightseeing

The main attractions of Chester are its ancient buildings. The **city walls**, built by the Romans and reinforced by the Normans, still stand, and, in fact, Chester is the only British city where the walls are wholly intact. Roman remains visible today are the ruins of an **amphitheatre** and the foundations of a large Roman building in the cellar of the shop at 28 Northgate Street. On the north and east side of the city, the walls follow the original Roman construction and incorporate their work. The north-eastern medieval tower is called the **King Charles Tower** because Charles I stood there to watch a Civil War battle in 1645.

The narrow streets in the city are called **Rows**. This is because there are rows of half timbered two-tiered shops all in a line that were built in the 1200s. If you follow Forgate Street eastwards and take the right fork at the roundabout, just beyond the Engine House pub, you will see an **ecumenical monument**. It marks the spot where Protestant George Marsh was burned to death by the Catholics in 1555. It also commemorates Saint John Plessington who was hanged, drawn and quartered in 1679 by the Protestants. His relics are venerated at the Franciscan church in Chester. Chester has a Cathedral and several churches. It also boasts the smallest racecourse in England. There is a wharf where you can hire a boat and explore the River Dee.

Sights Further Afield

Chester is close to North Wales and there is a good road along the coast. The model manufacturing village of **Sunshine,** built in 1888, is a short distance. William, Lord Leverhulme and his brother James, started a soap manufacturing company known to this day as Lever Bros. He introduced profit-sharing, pensions, medical care and other benefits for his employees.

The Best of Chester in Brief

Chester Cathedral. The original Norman church dates back to the early twelfth century and the Gothic Cathedral standing here was constructed in the fifteenth century. Highlights of the cathedral are its elegant and famous choir stalls, the refectory, the monastic cloisters and surrounding gardens. *St Werburgh Street.*

Grosvenor Museum. Delving into the days of Roman rule in the city, Chester's top museum has exhibits which vividly depict the social and military history of those times, with reconstructed buildings and a cemetery. Other drawcards are the art and craft galleries, Period House and the interactive displays. Keep an eye out for changing exhibitions. *27 Grosvenor Street.*

Chester Zoo. This is an award-winning regional zoo with some impressive facts and figures: it is Great Britain's largest garden zoo encompassing 50 hectares; contains 6000 animals representing more than 500 species, over half of which are on the endangered list; has a breeding colony for chimpanzees and a large herd of Asiatic elephants; and also has a Twilight Zone

Bat Cave, a Monkey Island exhibit, a Tropical Realm and a Zoofari Overhead Railway. *Upton-by-Chester*.

Chester Toy and Doll Museum. Children's toys of all kinds from the nineteenth and twentieth centuries fill five rooms. The museum is most famous for having the largest collection of Matchbox toys in the world. *13a Lower Bridge Street*.

Dewa Roman Experience. Focusing soley on Roman Chester, this museum goes to great lengths to show what it was like when the Romans walked the streets, with reconstructions filling in every detail of life. There is also an archaelogical exhibit. *Pierpoint Lane, Bridge Street*.

Bath

Bath is a quiet, sleepy city resting on the banks of the River Avon in South West England. It has a population of around 80,000.

History

The Romans founded a settlement here and named it Aquae Sulis because of its mineral springs. They turned it into a spa resort covering six acres with pools reaching temperatures of 49C (120F). They are still intact today.

After the Romans left, the Britons neglected the town and even built over some of the spa pools. The Roman baths were rediscovered in 1879. Bath became fashionable in the 18th century when famous people went there to "take the waters". Dickens, Swinburne, Defoe, Jane Austen and scores of other people of note found the soothing atmosphere conducive to inspiration.

Tourist Information

The Tourist Information Office is in the Abbey Churchyard, just south of the Abbey, and it is ☺open Mon-Sat 9.30am-5pm, Sun 10am-4pm, ✆(01225) 477 101 (rarely answered personally).

The office has a City Trail guidebook available for ✪£1.50, and it is worth its weight in gold for the serious visitor.

Local Transport

There are plenty of local buses that will take you to different points in the city, or you can take a tour bus to ensure that you will see all the points of interest.

Accommodation

Bath Spa

Sydney Road, BA2 6JF, ✆(01225) 444 424, fax 444 006. 98 rooms with all facilities. Georgian mansion built in 1850, renovated. Parking. Walking distance to all sights. 2 restaurants, bar - double ✪£150+.

The Francis on The Square, Queen Square, BA1 2HH, ✆(01225) 424 257, fax 319 715. 98 rooms with bath. Built in 1729. Overlooking Georgian Square, situated between Royal Crescent and the Abbey. Restaurant, bar - double ✪£100-150.

Athelney Guest House, 5 Marlborough Lane, Bath, ✆(01225) 312 031. 3 rooms, good meals - ✪£36-40.

Food and Drink

There are plenty of cafes and small restaurants, not to mention the pubs where food is served. The only alleged local delicacy is the Bath Bun, a type of sweet bread cake. It is available at many bakeries in the city, but the most popular place is rumoured to be *Mountstevens* on Westgate Street.

Bath Olivers are a biscuit that was originally invented to be eaten whilst "taking the waters", but the local factory that produced them was bombed during the war. Production has recommenced in Leamington Spa, and it is still recommended that they are at their best when eaten in a hot bath, even though they are now covered with chocolate. You can buy them from Waitrose supermarket in the Podium.

There is a cafe in North Parade Passage called **Sally Lunns** where they still bake the bun with the same name.

Since October 1997, Bath has again been brewing its own local beer, Abbey Ales. It is available from the Farmhouse on Lansdown Road.

Sightseeing

The Georgian nobles built elegant houses mostly in sweeping curves. The best example of this distinctive architecture is the **Royal Crescent**, an arc of thirty houses overlooking extensive lawns. House No. 1 is open to the public; No. 15 is the fictional home of Sir Percy Blakeney, the Scarlet Pimpernel. **The Circus**, where the houses are built in a circle is close by. Dr Livingstone lived at No. 13, and the painter Gainsborough at No. 17, where he painted the famous *Blue Boy*. As it is uphill, it is best to take a bus up to Royal Crescent and walk back down.

The ancient attractions are all in the centre of the city.

Next to the **Roman baths** are the **Pump Rooms**. Here you can have morning or afternoon tea served as one would imagine it being done in the 18th century. A string quartet plays music by the old masters. Thakeray used the Pump Room as one of the locations in *Vanity Fair*. The Roman Baths are ☉open Mon-Sat 9.30am-5pm, and there is an admission fee.

Bath Abbey, built in the 16th century, is famous for the stone angels on the facade. The carvings represent a dream of Bishop Oliver

King who built this last Tudor church before the Reformation. In his vision, angels climbed up and down ladders to heaven, but the only way the stonemasons could distinguish between the two was to make the ones descending do it head-first, which tends to make them look like 'fallen angels'. Inside, Australians would be interested in a memorial to Governor Philip who lived just off the Circus at 19 Bennett Street. The house bears a plaque.

Don't miss the **Pulteney Bridge**, with its elegant horseshoe-shaped weir. The bridge is one of only three in the world with shops on both its sides, and was designed by Robert Adam.

The **Museum of Costume**, which houses original garments since the late 1500s, is of interest to everyone not just those with an eye for fashion. It is housed in the *Assembly Rooms*, frequently mentioned by Jane Austen in her novels of early 19th century life.

Across the Avon in another 18th century building is the **Holbourne Museum and Crafts Study Centre**. It has a superb collection of 17th and 18th century art.

Sights Further Afield

For those with the time, a tour to Longleat, the home of the Marquise of Bath is worth a visit. The house is the finest example of Elizabethan architecture in the country. Built in 1550 it burnt down in 1567 and was rebuilt in 1572. The house is open all year round. There is also a lion safari park in the grounds.

The Best of Bath in Brief

Museum of Costume. This wonderful museum allows you to inspect the development of fashion from the sixteenth century to the present, decade by decade, with over 200 models dressed in detail down to jewelery and accessories. It is one of the top museums in Europe and arguably the best of its kind in the world. *Assembly Rooms, Bennett Street.*

 **Roman Baths**. These baths mark the origins of the city, where Romans discovered hot springs, were astonished by their soothing effects, and created their version of a resort town almost two thousand years ago. The great Roman temple, ancient uncovered treasures and the baths themselves are a must-see for a fascinating return to a past era. *Pump Room, Abbey Church Yard.*

Bath Abbey. This late fifteenth century abbey is built on the historical site where England's first King was crowned in an Anglo-Saxon abbey. Stained glass, fan vaulting and perpendicular Gothic architecture make it worth a second glance. *Abbey Church Yard.*

Industrial Heritage Cottage. A great collection of Victorian memorabilia.

Pump Room. Overlooking the King's Spring, the Grand Pump Room is an eighteenth century Georgian Hall in whose elegant interior you can sip your tea while relaxing to music played by the oldest resident trio in Europe. *Abbey Church Yard.*

Jane Austen Centre. Fans can retrace the esteemed author's daily footsteps, through her Georgian town house and along her favourite city paths, past sights made famous in her novels. *40 Gay Street, Queen Square.*

Assembly Rooms. This National Trust building functioned as a meeting and recreation hall in the eighteenth century. The chandeliers are originals from this time. *Bennett Street.*

Herschel House Museum. For astronomy buffs, this house was where Uranus was discovered back in 1781, on William Herschel's hand-made telescope. The modern NASA photographs here are offset by the preserved eighteenth century furniture. *19 New King Street.*

No 1 Royal Crescent. This restored Georgian house, with its fine Palladian architecture, dates back to 1774. It contains a museum highlighting some interesting features of Georgian life.

Stonehenge. Dated as far back as 3000BC, these mysterious stones, some weighing over 50 tonnes each, are thought to have been placed here by a neolithic people. The reasons for their circular placement and the method used to transport them are speculative. The dominant theory is that they form an ancient type of calendar and were rolled to the site on logs all the way from the Preseli Mountains in Wales, but nobody knows for sure. The engineering feat is staggering considering their age, and these mysterious stones have a unsettling and awe-inspiring ambience. *Located southeast of Bath in Amesbury, Wiltshire.*

Stratford-upon-Avon

Situated on the Avon River northwest of Oxford and London, the town made famous by William Shakespeare can be reached by car in about 2 hours from the capital.

This is 'Shakespeareville'. From names of restaurants to T-shirts, the playwright's most famous lines live on, four hundred years after his death, in no greater concentration than here.

Tourist Information

The tourist information office is in Bridge Street, ✆293 127, ⊙open 9.00am to 5.00pm. They can help with accommodation but will charge a service fee. The area code is 01789.

Sightseeing

You can purchase a number of combination tickets from the Tourist Office. The best is the one that covers the main sights you want to see - where Shakespeare was born, lived and was buried - and it costs about ✪£8.00.

Shakespeare's Birthplace, Henley Street. ⊙Open Monday to Sunday 10.00am to 4.00pm. A good museum for those interested in his life and work. Get there early to avoid crowds. Cost ✪£6.00.

New Place, on High Street, is where the playwright lived. Only the foundations remain.

Holy Trinity Church, on Trinity Street, houses his grave. The cost for the privelage of saying you have been to Will's resting place is ✪£1.00.

Presumably you have come here to see a Shakespearean performance by the **Royal Shakespeare Company**. Bookings can be made at the box office in the foyer of Royal Shakespeare Theatre on Waterside, ✆403 403. If you only want to hear what's on, find out the availability of tickets at following costs ✪£20, £15, £5 and how to book, ✆403 404 has a recorded message. ⊙Open 9.00am to 8.00pm Monday to Saturday. They tend to be evening performances so you may have to plan to stay in town overnight.

Sights Further Afield

Warwick Castle is a fine Medieval Castle that has been turned into a living museum of medieval times. ⊙Open daily from 10.00am to 4.00pm. Cost ✪£12. Twenty minutes by train (Cost £5.00 round trip) from Stratford.

Oxford

Oxford can be visited on a day excursion from London, or as a stopover on the way to other interesting places further west. The journey is some 90 minutes by bus.

Oxford houses over 30 colleges which have educated the (privileged) youth of England and other parts of the globe since the time of Henry II. Though encroached upon by commerce and industry, Oxford has that special flavour enhanced by the student population which tends to give life to any urban area. The colleges of Oriel, Magdalen, Christ, Jesus, Balliol, Pembroke, Queens, and so on, have their own ethos, specialties and standards. Magnificent stone structures replete with imposing gargoyles give way to manicured lawns and rather strange security men. If, as you peer through the wall portals at one of the well-tended lawns, you are approached by someone in a top hat and black suit who asks 'Can I help you, sir?', what he really means is 'Get lost'.

Tributaries of the River Thames surround the University and add to the pleasant ambience. Most afternoons you can come across rowers out training in the skiffs with the coxswain calling out the time, and on weekends (more so than weekdays) couples are out 'punting' (a narrow boat steered and propelled forward by a long oar) up and down the river. More often than not the days are either wet or overcast, however, if you strike a sunny day, the town and university are resplendent.

Tourist Information

The Tourist Information Office is at Gloucester Green, ℂ7260871, fax 240 261 and at the Railway Station. They can book accommodation for you but will charge a fee. They have an excellent guide map for 60p. ☺Open Monday to Saturday 9.30am to 5.00pm, Sunday 10am to 3.30pm. The telephone area code is 01865.

How to Get There

By Train - from Paddington Station every 30 minutes and ostensibly it takes one hour. Cost is ✪£14.80 return.

By Bus - this is the best and most effective way to get to Oxford. *Oxford City Link*, ✆785 400 (in Oxford) runs from Gloucester Green (it is a paved square - no grass here) off George Street in Oxford to Victoria Station, London. There are designated stops in London - the bus goes up Bayswater Road so you can get off near your hotel if you are staying in that part of London. Cost ✪£7.50. Takes 1 3/4 hours. Leaves every 15 minutes.

Sightseeing

Christ Church Chapel is ☺open 9.30am to 5.00pm (entry ✪£2.50) and from the tower you get a view of Oxford, which can also be obtained from the Carfax Tower (✪£1.50) in Cornmarket Street. The **Bodleian Library** is the main library of the university (☺open 9am to 6.00pm) and next to it is the oval-shaped **Sheldon Theatre** (☺open 10am to noon, 2.30pm to 4.00pm, charge). Further away but worth a visit is the **Ashmolean Museum** in Beaumont Street that houses works by many of the masters from Da Vinci to Monet. *Blackwell's Bookstore* on Broad Street is worth a visit. Once the ultimate in bookstores, you can judge for yourself how well it has weathered the amazon.com challenge of recent years. For book buffs it is a must.

As you are in *the* University town (although Cambridge-folk may disagree) you should take time to see a university College. **Magdalen**, down High Street and near the River, with its extensive grounds and its amazing stone lace work, is worth a visit. ☺Open Monday to Friday 2pm to 5.00pm, sometimes later in summer, cost ✪£2.00. Students from other universities enter free. Be prepared to show some identification.

Food and Drink

This is a university town, so the restaurants and the entertainment are geared to the needs of the majority. There are a lot of pubs.

Shopping

Memorabilia can be purchased from shops in the covered market near Market Street.

Accommodation

Accommodation can be obtained through the Tourist Information office. There is a YHA Youth Hostel in Jack Straw's Lane, ✆762 997, which is out of the main area and a bit of a hike. An alternative is Backpackers Hotel, Hythe Bridge Street, ✆721 761, or one of many B&B's on the outskirts of town. There are also some three star hotels, and the major chains are well represented nearby.

One place with character that is often recommended is **Bath Place** in the middle of town, ✆018 650791 812. Cost is around ✪£80-125 depending on the season.

Sights Further Afield

You can use Oxford as a base to visit **Blenheim Palace** - ✆01993 811 091, ⊙open March to October 11.00am to 5.00pm, entry is ✪£10 - by bus from Oxford (Gloucester Green). Stagecoach Express buses charge ✪£4 return and run every half hour. The palace is only 10 miles away so the bus trip takes less than 30 minutes. The Tourist Information centre at Gloucester Green where you buy your ticket can give you more detailed information.

Cambridge

A trip to Cambridge is recommended as a day excursion from London.

Unlike Oxford, Cambridge does little to encourage the tourists. The town is smaller than Oxford - less than 110,000 people - and though it is set attractively on the River Cam running past, one gets the impression that this old Benedictine centre of learning is determined to stay that way.

If you are driving into Cambridge, take note of the 'rising bollards'. Certain parts of the town proper and the university are strictly pedestrian-only, except for those who carry a permit. Bollards are poles which stand upright in the road and are activated to descend if you have the right pass. Some Australian tourists witnessed a little old mini go across the bollards, which had obligingly withdrawn, only to see them rise immediately beneath the unauthorised Renault following behind. The French couple were left suspended in the air, stranded until help arrived. So 'beware the rising bollards'.

Like Oxford, this is a university town with a lot of life, and the pubs, bars and restaurants cater accordingly to their clientele.

Tourist Information

The tourist office is in Wheeler Street, ©322 640, fax 457 588, ®www.cambridge.gov.uk/leisure/tourism. They can book rooms for a fee. ☺Open Monday to Saturday 10.00am to 5.00pm. They can also direct you to cybercafes if wish to access email accounts.

Guided Tours - these are certainly recommended for King's College and the Fitzwilliam Museum. A fee is charged - about ✪£4.00 and it is worth it, unless you have a friend who can show you around and is an expert in all the social and historical details of the places you see and visit.

The telephone area code is 01223.

How to Get There

By Train - Cambridge is on the King's Lynn line. Board at Liverpool or King Cross Station in London. They run every half and hour and the trip takes one hour twenty minutes. Cost is ✪£15 return.

By Bus - From Drummer Street between Emmanuel and Christ College. National Express to Victoria Station, London - every 20 minutes, ✪£8.50. Trip takes about 2 hours.

Sightseeing

King's College. The architecture of this place is stunning, highlighted by the Gothic architecture of King's College Chapel, almost 70 years in the making. *The Adoration of the Magi* by Rubens hangs inside. The college is ☺open from Monday to Friday 9.30am to 5.00pm. Tours of the Chapel can be arranged by the tourist office, ✪£3.50.

The Wren Library in Trinity College houses many notable treasures, not the least of which is the stunning architectural decoration of the place itself. ☺Open Monday to Saturday noon to 2pm. Closed during exams. Fee charged.

Fitzwilliam Museum is just south of Peterhouse on Trumpington Street which becomes the A10 heading towards London. It houses many Egyptian, Greek and Chinese treasures which the Brits plundered during their many wanderings and conquests in past eras. They also have some Japanese pieces that must have been obtained by more orderly means. ☺Open Monday to Saturday 10.00am to 5.00pm, Sunday 2.30pm to 5.00pm (hardly worth the visit). Fee charged ✪£3.00.

Edinburgh

The city of Edinburgh is the capital of Scotland and the second largest city, with a population of around 420,000. Nowadays it is a cultural centre thanks in the main to the very popular *Edinburgh Festival*. The magnificent Edinburgh castle overlooks the city protectively.

History

Strategically placed on the shores of the Firth of Forth, Edinburgh played an important part in the wars between England and Scotland in medieval times. After the death of Elizabeth I of England, James VI of

Scotland also became James I of England and moved his court south, causing Edinburgh to lose some of its importance. In recent years this has been regained by its contribution to learning.

Tourist Information

Scottish Tourist Board, 23 Ravelston Terrace, Edinburgh, ©(0131) 332 2433, fax 315 4545 (☞www.holiday.scotland.net/os).

Local Transport

There are plenty of buses to all parts of the city. In the city centre it is better to walk.

Accommodation

Following is a selection of accommodation with prices for a double room per night, which should be used as a guide only.

Best Western Apex International, 31-35 Grassmarket, Edinburgh, EH1 2HS, ©(0131) 300 3456, fax 220 5345. Located in historic Old Town. 175 rooms, rooftop restaurant with great views of the castle, bar, lounge - ✪£120-180.

Carlton Highland Hotel, North Bridge, Edinburgh, EH1 1SD, ©(0131) 472 3000, fax 556 2691 (✉travelweb@hotelbook.com(08504)). In the heart of the Royal Mile. 4-star facilities including a restaurant and night club - ✪£75-193.

Albany Town House Hotel

39 Albany Street, Edinburgh, EH1 3QY, ©(0131) 556 0397, fax 557 6633 (✉travelweb@hotelbook.com(28770)). A superior first class hotel situated in the New Town. Has a restaurant and bar - ✪£75-185.

Quality Hotel Commodore-Edinburgh, Marine Drive, Edinburgh, EH4 5EP, ℂ(0131) 336 1700, fax 336 4934. Restaurant, cocktail bar - ✪£75-108.

Best Western Braid Hills Hotel, 134 Braid Road, Edinburgh, EH10 6JD, ℂ(0131) 447 8888, fax 452 8477. Built in 1886 for golfers visiting Braid Hills Courses nearby. Good location for visiting all the attractions of Edinburgh. 67 rooms, bar/lounge, restaurant - ✪£70-110.

Tulip Jarvis Learmonth, 18-20 Learmonth Terrace, Edinburgh, EH4 1PW, ℂ(0131) 343 2671, fax 315 2232 (✉travelweb@hotelbook. com(25854)). Situated half a mile from the city centre, one and a half miles from the Castle. 62 rooms, restaurant with extensive menu, terrace bar - £65-119.

Quality Hotel Edinburgh Airport, 1 Ingliston, Edinburgh, EH28 8NF, ℂ(0131) 333 4331, fax 333 4124. Bar/lounge, restaurant - ✪£55-105.

Simpsons Hotel, 79 Lauriston Place, Edinburgh, ℂ(0131) 622 7979, fax 622 7900 (✉travelweb@hotelbook.com(29540)). Centrally situated with 57 rooms, bar - ✪£49-100.

Food and Drink

The Scots have a dish called *haggis* which is delicious although some people steer clear of it because of the recipe. It consists of oatmeal, minced offal, suet and seasoning, cooked in maw (the stomach of a sheep).

Seafood is one specialty and oyster bars are plentiful. Others are Scotch whisky, smoked haddock, salmon, kippers, herrings, and cock-a-leekie soup, which is made from a whole fowl and leeks with other seasonings. Dunlop Cheese has a rich, mellow flavour. Another very local dish is "tatties an' herrin" (potatoes and herring boiled together).

Shopping

The best buys are tweed materials. Tweed made into garments is very popular and quite unique. Fine woollen items, silk shawls, worsteds and linen are also popular.

Sightseeing

Taking a tour on the jump on/jump off double-decker buses is always a good way to get your bearings in a new city. The tour of Edinburgh takes about an hour in total, and buses leave from central locations about every 15 minutes.

Edinburgh Castle dominates the city, and the best view of it is from Princes Street. Inside the castle you can inspect the apartments occupied by Mary Queen of Scots, including the room where she gave birth to James I. The **Crown Jewels**, which  were recovered by Sir Walter Scott, are also kept here. There is also a collection of antique weapons, the banqueting hall and a military museum. At ☉1pm each day a cannon is fired, a 150 year tradition. Other attractions within the castle are the 11th century **St Margaret's Chapel**, **Old Parliament Hall**, and the small cemetery containing the remains of military mascots (dogs). There is a changing of the guard ceremony, but it is the antithesis of those that take place at Buckingham Palace, being instead very relaxed, with the participants obviously enjoying themselves.

The **National War Memorial** stands close by. The **Royal Mile** is a cobbled street lined with interesting shops and houses, including one that was occupied by John Knox, founder of the Calvinist Presbyterian Church in Scotland in 1560. Below the Castle is a wide parade ground where the Edinburgh Tattoo is held.

At the end of the road stands the palace of **Holyrood House**. It is the Queen's official residence but visitors can inspect it when she is not staying there. Inside there are many antiquities including needlework done by Mary Queen of Scots. A plaque commemorates the place where her secretary Rizzio was murdered on the instructions of Queen Mary's husband, Lord Darnley.

There are many small streets running off the Royal Mile.

In **Lawnmarket** stands the six storey tenement house built in 1620, and known as Gladstone's Land. It is furnished in the style of a merchant's house of the time, and the ceilings are magnificently painted. Nearby is **Lady Stair's House** a town dwelling of 1622. It has exhibits by Sir Walter Scott, Robert Louis Stevenson and Robbie Burns. In High Street the Cathedral called **The High Kirk of St Giles** dates from the 12th century.

Canongate was once a separate burgh outside the walls of Edinburgh.

Huntley House, built in 1520, is a museum featuring Edinburgh's history and social life. The most impressive structure along **Princes Street** is the 60m statue of Sir Walter Scott. Not far away are the **National Gallery**, **Zoological Park**, **Parliament House**, **Greyfriars Churchyard**, **Museum of Childhood** and the **Royal Scottish Museum**.

Sights Further Afield

Three miles from the city is **Craigmillar Castle**, while not far from the city is the ancient seaport and castle of **Dunbar** and the fashionable resort of **North Berwick**.

The Best of Edinburgh in Brief

Royal Mile. This historic stretch makes for a wonderful walk for any visitor to Edinburgh. Highlights are the Castle Esplanade at the bottom of which is a site where many witches were burnt at the stake for about two-and-a-half centuries; Gladstone's Land, a sixteenth century merchant's house; Writers' Museum, in a sixteenth century house called Lady Stair's House which displays manuscripts by some famous Scottish authors and poets; St Giles Cathedral, the most important church in the country; Tron Kirk, housing an historical display of the city; John Knox House, containing a museum of the life of the Presbyterian Church's founder; People's Story, an exhibition dedicated to the working class produced by the Industrial Revolution; and Holyrood Palace, the once-a-year residence of the Queen when she visits Scotland.

Edinburgh Castle. The 1300-year-old fortress dominating the skyline atop the hill and overlooking sprawling Edinburgh below has some wonderful views and must-see attractions inside. The Great Hall, the Scottish National War Memorial, St. Margaret's Chapel and the Scottish Crown Jewels are not to be missed. *Castlehill*.

Walter Scott Monument. This soaring monument, with great views from its peak, is topped by a marble statue of the Scottish author and decorated with the likenesses of actual poets and fictional characters. *East Princes Street Gardens*.

National Gallery of Scotland. The best collection of Scottish paintings anywhere, and also some surprising masterpeices by European greats such as Raphael and Titian. *2 The Mound*.

Scottish National Gallery of Modern Art. A plethora of twentieth century art from a varied and terrific selection of well-known modern artists. *Belford Road*.

Glasgow

Glasgow on the River Clyde, is the largest city in Scotland and the third largest city in the United Kingdom, with a population of around 760,000. It is a relatively modern city, and not many buildings pre-date the Victorian era. Its once depressed areas, including the Gorbals, have long been levelled and replaced.

History

Glasgow was a religious and learning centre in the 12th century. Shipbuilding was always one of its major industries, but it has now declined. Both the great ships the *Queen Mary* and the *Queen Elizabeth* were built along the River Clyde. Other industries include engineering, textiles, brewing, chemicals and whisky blending. Glasgow grew rapidly after 1707 when Scotland was united with England. It was the chief port for the importation of tobacco and sugar from the New World.

The city survived the industrial revolution with its deposits of coal and iron ore nearby.

Tourist Information

The Greater Glasgow & Clyde Valley Tourist Board, 11 George Square, Glasgow G2 1DY, ©(0141) 204 4400, fax 221 3524, (☞www. seeglasgow.com, ✎tourismglasgow@ggcvth.org.uk).

Local Transport

Buses are plentiful. Tours are also available.

Accommodation

Following is a selection of accommodation with prices for a double room per night, which should be used as a guide only.

> ### *Copthorne Glasgow*
>
> George Square, Glasgow, GS IDS, ℭ(0141) 332 6711, fax 332 4264 (✎travelweb@ hotelbook.com(03847)). A good location, situated in the centre of the city and convenient for sightseers and business travellers with a tight schedule. 140 rooms, restaurant, bar. It is a stylish hotel with an attractive facade and an interior to match. Room decor and facilities are not overly luxurious, but they are adequate and suited to the price range - ✪£107-135.

Thistle Glasgow, 36 Cambridge Street, Glasgow, G2 3HN, ℭ(0141) 332 3311, fax 332 4050 (✎glasgow@thistle.co.uk). Scotland's largest conference hotel. 302 rooms, 2 restaurants, 2 bars - ✪£105-140.

Jarvis Ingram Hotel, 201 Ingram Street, Glasgow, G1 IDQ, ℭ(0141) 248 4401, fax 226 5913 (✎travelweb@hotelbook.com(29571)). In the city centre near the Cathedral. 91 rooms, bar and grill with an extensive menu - ✪£86-94.

Quality Hotel Central-Glasgow, 99 Gordon Street, Glasgow, G1 3SF, ℭ(0141) 221 9680, fax 226 3948. Bar/lounge, restaurant, indoor pool - ✪£75-108.

Black Bull Thistle Hotel, Main Street, Glasgow, G62, 6BH, ℭ(0141) 956 2291, fax 956 1896 (✎reservations@thistle.co.uk). Situated outside Glasgow in proximity to Loch Lomond and the Trossachs. 27 rooms, restaurant, 3 bars - ✪£77-93.

Buchanan Hotel, 185 Buchanan Street, Glasgow, G1 2JY, ✆(0141) 332 7284, fax 333 0635. Situated in the heart of the city, only yards from Royal Concert Hall. 59 rooms, bar/lounge, restaurant - ✪£60-95.

Bruce Hotel, Cornwall Street, East Kilbride, Glasgow, G74 1AF, ✆(01355) 229 771, fax 242 216 (✉travelweb@hotelbook.com (28856)). In the city centre adjoining the Plaza Shopping Centre. 110 rooms - ✪£60-90.

Food and Drink

Good wholesome food is readily available. Some restaurants serve continental fare. Seafood, smoked and fresh salmon, and haggis are local specialties.

Shopping

Glasgow has one of the finest shopping thoroughfares in Britain - **Sauchiehall Street**. You can buy almost anything there.

Sightseeing

St Munro's Cathedral dates from the 12th century. **Glasgow University** was built in 1451. Other places of interest are: **Kelvingrove Art Gallery and Museum** houses a fine collection of European art including Salvador Dali's famous painting of the *Crucifixion*; **The Museum of Transport** includes a re-creation of a 1938 street; **The Glasgow School of Art** was designed by Charles Rennie Mackintosh and contains much of his work. The **Burrell Art Collection** is housed in a gallery in Pollock Park.

Glasgow also has the biggest football stadium in Britain, **Hampden Park**. In 1989, at **Culcreuch Castle**, a short distance north of Glasgow, Tom Moody, an Australian cricketer, won a haggis-throwing competition with a throw of 67m, beating the local record of 50m.

Sights Further Afield

A short distance from Glasgow are some of the most scenic areas in the whole of Scotland. **Loch Lomond**, is one of the most beautiful lakes in Europe. It can be reached in less than an hour. Trips are usually extended into the loch and mountainous country of **Argyle**. The road travels through the charming little town of **Inveraray** where the Duke of Argyle, Chief of the Clan Campbell, has his castle.

On the Atlantic side of Glasgow, the sea-lochs cleave deep into the mountains. The wild scenery of **Loch Long**, one of the longest, deepest and most beautiful fjords is easily accessible. Charming **Loch Goil** is right on Glasgow's doorstep.

The Best of Glasgow in Brief

Bothwell Castle. Scotland's greatest thirteenth century stone castle is set attractively above the Clyde and has a tumultuous history. *Castle Avenue, Uddington.*

Burrell Collection. This collection has a variety of artifacts, including sculpture and tapestries, representing chiefly the ancient, classical and medieval eras. *2060 Pollockshaws Road.*

Gallery of Modern Art. A unique contemporary gallery whose four floors are divided thematically into the four natural elements. *Queen Street.*

Glasgow Botanic Gardens. Highlights in these gardens are the many tropical plants and the Victorian Kibble Palace with its marble statues. *730 Great Western Road.*

Glasgow Cathedral. The city's patron saint, St Mungo, is buried in the crypt of this twelfth century Gothic cathedral. *Castle Street.*

Hunterian Art Gallery. An outstanding collection of works from the seventeenth century onwards, taking in paintings by Rembrandt, portraits, Scottish works, American art and modern sculpture. *University of Glasgow, 82 Hillhead Street*.

Hunterian Museum. Scotland's oldest museum, this musuem has a great array of pieces including the Bearsden Shark which is 330 million years old, dinosaur bones, coins, archaelogical treasures, scientific instruments, medals, maps and much more. *University of Glasgow, University Avenue*.

Museum of Transport. All modes of transport are represented in this rare collection of transport memorabilia. *Kelvin Hall, 1 Bunhouse Road*.

People's Palace Museum. Two hundred years of Glaswegian history and culture is recounted in a vibrant and modern style. *Glasgow Green*.

University of Glasgow Visitor Centre. The Visitors Centre of the fourth oldest university in the United Kingdom contains interactive displays with cutting-edge technology. *University Avenue*.

Belfast

Belfast is the Capital of Northern Ireland, which, for trivia buffs, is part of the United Kingdom but not of Great Britain, the latter referring only to England, Scotland and Wales. The city is situated on the banks of the River Lagan, where it flows into the Belfast Lough on the border of Counties Antrim and Down. The surrounding hills are soft and green, so typical of the scenery of Northern Ireland. It has a population of around 400,000.

History

Belfast became a city in 1888. Around the turn of the century it was the biggest ship-building centre in the world, its most famous vessel being the *Titanic*. In 1921 it became the capital of the newly created Northern Ireland. In 1969, due to sectarian violence, the British sent the military in, and tourists stayed away in their thousands. It is only in the last few years, mainly since the Good Friday peace Accord in 1998, that Belfast is back on travel itineraries.

Tourist Information

The Tourism Development Office, Belfast City Council, The Cecil Ward Building, 4-10 Linenhall Street, Belfast, BT2 8BP, ℂ(01232) 320 202 ext 3585.

Local Transport

Local public transport is good. Ask at your hotel or the local tourist information.

Accommodation

Following is a selection of accommodation with prices for a double room per night, which should be used as a guide only.

Belfast Hilton International Hotel, 4 Lanyon Place, Belfast, BT1 2LP, ℂ(01232) 277000, fax 277 277 (✉travelweb@hotelbook.com (28732)). A 5-star hotel situated in the heart of the city overlooking the River Lagan. 195 rooms, restaurant, bar/lounge - ✪£155-203.

Europa Hotel, Great Victoria Street, Belfast, BT2 7AP, ℂ(01232) 327 000, fax 327 800 (✉travelweb@hotelbook.com(00047)). Famous hotel in the heart of Belfast. 184 rooms, restaurant, lounge/bar, brasserie - ✪£99-140.

Quality Hotel Fergus, 75 Belfast Road, Carrickfergus, BT 38 8PH, ℂ(02893) 364 556, fax 351 620. Restaurant, bar/lounge - ✪£85-150.

Stormont Hotel, 587 Upper Newtownards Road, County Down, Belfast, BT4 34P, ℰ(01232) 658 621, fax 480 240 (✓travelweb@ hotelbook.com(20778)). Situated half a mile from Stormont Castle, and 4 miles from Belfast city centre. 109 rooms, 2 restaurants, bar/lounge - ✪£60-130.

Jury's Belfast Inn, Great Victoria Street, Belfast Antrim, Belfast, BT2 7AP, ℰ(01232) 533 500, fax 533 511 (✓travelweb@hotelbook. com(25814)). Situated opposite the Opera House and City Hall. 191 rooms, coffee shop, lounge - ✪£55-63.

Food and Drink

Main restaurants offer continental and British specialties but the Irish prefer plain hearty meals of meat, bread and vegetables. Fish and chips and home baked bread made from whole-wheat flour are specialities. Try the pubs for a good meal at a reasonable price.

Shopping

Best buys are Belfast linen and Irish whiskey.

Men's shirts and collars made in Londonderry are world renowned for their quality.

Sightseeing

The city centre is dominated by the copper dome of the **City Hall**, in Donegall Square, which was modelled on St Paul's Cathedral in London. Free guided tours are available ☉Oct-May Mon-Sat 2.30pm, June-Sept Mon-Fri 10.30am, 11.30am, 2.30pm, Sat 2.30pm only, ℰ(01232) 270 405 for recorded information.

Another landmark of the city is **Belfast Castle**, which is 400 ft above sea level on the slopes of Cave Hill. The first castle on this site was built by the Normans in the late 12th century, then in 1611 a stone and timber castle was erected. The present building was commenced in 1862 by the 3rd Marquis of Donegall, but his fortune had dwindled dramatically before the building was finished, and his son-in-law, Lord Ashley, heir to the title Earl of Shaftesbury, had to step in and meet the shortfall. In 1884 the 3rd Marquis died, and in 1885 the 7th Earl of Shaftesbury followed, and Lord Ashley and his wife inherited the Shaftesbury title and the Donegall home.

The castle was presented to the City of Belfast in 1934, and from the end of the 2nd World War to the 1970s, it was a venue for wedding receptions, dances and afternoon teas. In 1978, the Belfast City Council began a major refurbishment program, and the building was officially re-opened to the public in 1988.

The castle's cellars were opened in 1990, having been transformed into a Victorian atmosphere of narrow streets, shop fronts, gas lights, and the like. Visitors can now enjoy an antique and craft shop, the **Castle Tavern** bar and the **Castle Kitchen** - a bistro that is ☉open daily and serves everything from light snacks to full meals.

From the summit of **Cave Hill**, on a clear day, you can see the Isle of Man and the Ayreshire coast.

Belfast Zoo, Antrim Road, on the side of Cave Hill, offers great views of the city. It has all the usual animals and is ☉open April-Sept daily 10am-5pm, Oct-March Sat-Thurs 10am-3.30pm, Fri 10am-2.30pm. There is an entry fee, ✆(01232) 776 277.

Linenhall Library, Donegall Square, opposite City Hall, has been lending books out since 1788. It is ☉open Mon-Wed, Fri 9.30am-5.30pm, Thurs 9.30am-8.30pm, Sat 9.30am-4.30pm, ✆(01232) 321 707. Even if you don't want to borrow a book, you can enjoy a quiet cup of coffee upstairs.

Parliament met in Belfast from 1921-1972 then moved to **Stormont**, five miles outside the city. The dignified building where it now meets is made of Portland stone and was opened in 1932 by the then Prince of Wales. Nearby is the Prime Minister's House.

The **Queen's University** received a Royal Charter in 1909, and is situated in the south of Belfast, near the **Botanic Gardens**, the **Palm House**, which has many exotic plants, and the **Ulster Museum**, ☺open Mon-Fri 10am-5pm, Sat 1-5pm, Sun 2-5pm, ✆(01232) 383 000. The centrepiece of the museum is the *Girona Treasure*, which consists of relics recovered in the 1960s from three Spanish Armada vessels which sank off the coast in 1588. Admission is free.

The **Ulster Folk Museum** consists of farmhouses, watermills, a whole village, shops and church, all moved from the countryside and reassembled here. Across the road is the **Transport Museum**. For opening hours of both museums, ✆(01232) 428 428.

Mount Stewart House and Gardens are rated by the National Trust in the top six in the UK.

Along the north bank of **Belfast Lough** stands a small community called **Carrickfergus**. Here the ancestors of Andrew Jackson, President of the USA, kept an inn. On the waterfront stands an inscribed stone to commemorate the landing of King William III who was on his way to defeat James I at the Battle of the Boyne. Within sight of Carrickfergus' ancient castle and in the Belfast Lough, Captain John Paul Jones, a Scottish gardener ran up his colours on the *Ranger* and fought it out with HMS *Drake*. He was one of the founders of the US Navy.

Giant's Ring is a circular rampart 200m in diameter that may be as much as 4000 years old. It is a mile south of Shaw's Bridge, off the N23.

Sights Further Afield

One of the most picturesque and scenic highways in Europe is a winding road running north from Belfast along the coast. At times the road is so close to the water that the windscreen is covered with spray. The highway crosses rocky peninsulas with views of basalt highlands and the deep waters of the Irish Sea. Well worth the time it takes.

The Best of Belfast in Brief

City Hall. Constructed at the turn of the nineteenth century, this proud building contains a statue of Queen Victoria, a marble staircase, the original charter of Belfast from the early seventeenth century, and the Great Hall. *Howard Street*.

Falls Road. Although things have certainly calmed down by comparison with former days, a visitor to this corner of town can sense (or imagine) the tension of sectarian violence and discontent still crackling in the air. The area has the Peace Line, the headquarters of Sinn Fein and a commemorative IRA cemetery.

Botanic Gardens. A lovely park setting with a Tropical Ravine and Palm House on the grounds.

Ulster Museum. Apart from an Egyptian mummy, the Girona Treasure and a medieval exhibit, there is little else to thrill visitors to this museum. *University Road*.

Driving Through Great Britain

You could easily spend a month touring around England, Scotland and Wales.

England

Itinerary - 12 Days - Distance 1450kms

After spending time exploring **London**, head north east to **Cambridge**. Cambridge is a famous university town, with many historic buildings. From here, drive north to **Lincoln**. This city dates

from Roman times, and there are many interesting ruins. The cathedral is spectacular.

Further north of Lincoln, you reach **York**, a preserved medieval walled city, and famous for the York Minster. There are also interesting museums here. Head north, through the Yorkshire Dales, stopping at small towns such as **Ripon** and **Richmond**. Richmond is a good starting point for visiting the National Park. Continue on to **Hexham**, which is close to Hadrians Wall. This was started in the 1st century. The Northumberland Dales are also near here.

Continue on to **Edinburgh**, the capital of Scotland. Here there are many things to see and do, including making a visit to the famous Edinburgh Castle. Each August the Edinburgh Festival is held, and the Military Tattoo is popular. From Edinburgh head south towards the Lake District. On the way you pass through towns such as **Peebles**, famous for its salmon fishing, and **Selkirk**, with its links to Queen Victoria and Sir Walter Scott.

On the border, **Gretna Green** used to be a popular place for eloping couples to marry. **Windermere**, **Keswick** and **Grasmere** all lie in the heart of the Lake District. This picturesque area is very popular as a holiday destination. The poet Wordsworth lived at Grasmere, and you can visit the museum in his honour. Drive south from here until you reach **Blackpool**, a typical English seaside resort.

Continue south to **Chester**, a medieval walled city with relics dating from Roman times. There are many historic buildings here. From Chester, head west along the north coast of Wales, stopping at coastal towns such as **Colwyn Bay** and **Bangor**. **Caernavon** is famous for its castle, dating from the 13th century. The Snowdonia National Park is ideal for day and longer walks, and is accessible from here.

Head south east over the Cambrian Mountains to **Shrewesbury**. This town is located on both sides of the Severn River, and is an appealing sight with its black and white timbered houses. From here, drive to **Stratford-upon-Avon**, Shakespeare's birth place and a very popular tourist destination. You must book well in advance for theatre bookings at the Royal Shakespeare Theatre.

Further south, you reach **Oxford**, another famous old university town, with many historic buildings still in use today. Make your way back through the picturesque Chilterns to London where your tour finishes.

The South of England

Itinerary - 10 Days - Distance 1002kms

From **London**, drive west to **Windsor**, famous for the castle - home of the Royal Family. Many parts of the castle are open for public entry. Windsor is also noted for its Safari Park, and Eton Public School, one of the oldest in England. Head south west to **Salisbury**. Salisbury Cathedral is well known as one of the most beautiful cathedrals in the United Kingdom. A copy of the Magna Carta is held here. Close by Salisbury lies **Stonehenge**, with ancient stone circles dating from 2200 BC. It is no longer possible to wander through these huge stone pillars. From here head north to **Bath** and **Bristol**. Bath is an elegant

Stonehenge, southeast of Bath

spa town, with relics dating from Roman times. Bristol is a lively city, situated on the river Severn.

Make your way south through the cathedral city of **Wells** to **Glastonbury**. This town is famous for being the first place where Christianity was practised in England, in AD 700. **Exeter** lies on the southern coast. This is a good starting point for touring Devon and Cornwall. Exeter, an old Roman town was overrun by Norman troops, and the remains of William the Conqueror's castle can still be seen. The Maritime Museum is a reminder of the towns naval history.

Travel east now along the south coast, through seaside resorts such as **Lyme Regis** and **Bournemouth**. Drive through the New Forest town of **Lyndhurst**. Wild horses still run free in the forest. The port cities of **Southampton** and **Portsmouth** provide access to the Isle of Wight. Make a detour to **Winchester**, once the capital of England, with its beautiful cathedral. The Great Hall of the castle reputedly contains King Arthur's round table.

Continue along the coast to **Brighton**, another popular holiday destination. The Indian inspired Royal Palace is worth visiting. **Folkestone** and **Dover** are important ferry ports for crossing to the continent. Head north from Dover to **Canterbury**. The first Canterbury Cathedral was started in the 11th century. The town is full of history and there are many interesting museums. Head back to London through the pleasant Kent countryside.

The Highlands of Scotland

Itinerary - 11 Days - Distance 1447kms

After spending time in **Edinburgh**, head north to the coast and the famous **St Andrews** golf course. Unless you have reciprocal club membership, tourists must go into a ballot to be entitled to play golf on this course. Drive north to **Perth**, the old capital of Scotland, with its historic buildings. From Perth head towards **Braemar**, where the Highland Games are held each August. Balmoral Castle, summer residence of the Royal Family is nearby.

Aberdeen lies on the east coast of Scotland, and is associated with the North Sea oil industry. To the north west of Aberdeen, in the Speyside region, you find the centre of the whisky industry. Many of the distilleries are open to the public. Continue on to Inverness, where the nearby Loch Ness is well known for its monster. From **Inverness**, take the coastal road to **John O'Groats**, the northern most point of Scotland. From here you can see across to the Orkney Islands.

Head west along the coast to the remote town of **Durness**, and then down the rugged western coastline to **Ullapool**, where ferries depart for the Outer Hebrides. Another ferry port leading to the Isle of Skye is at **Kyle of Lochalsh**. From here make your way south to **Fort William** at the foot of Ben Nevis, and **Glencoe**, the site of the massacre of the McDonald clan by the Campbells. Head back past Loch Lomond to **Stirling**, where the restored castle is impressive, to complete your trip in Edinburgh.

Ireland

THE LUSH, GREEN ISLAND is off the west coast of Britain and has an area of 68,893 sq km with a population of around 4,000,000. It is joined to Northern Ireland and occupies five-sixths of the entire land mass. Its Irish name is Eire but in 1949 it changed its name to The Republic of Ireland. It became a member of the EEC in 1973. The capital is Dublin. The official languages are English and Irish (Gaeilge), but English is mainly spoken.

Ireland, though an an agricultural country with beautiful scenery, is making a name for itself in the software and information technology industries. It is also noted for the breeding of fine thoroughbred horses.

Climate

Ireland has a moderate climate where the mild south-westerly winds prevail. The Gulf Stream keeps the waters warm. January and February are the coldest months and July and August the warmest. Average temperatures are 39F (4C) -60F (16C). It is advisable to pack a warm jumper and raincoat.

Entry Regulations

A valid passport is necessary. For an extended stay, contact your nearest Irish Embassy.

Duty free allowance is 200 cigarettes or 100 cigarillos or 50 cigars. 1 litre of alcohol over 22% or 2 litres of alcohol not exceeding 22% 2 litres of still wine, 50gm perfume 0.25 litres toilet water. Goods to the value of IR£34. A maximum of 25 litres of beer may be imported as part of the above allowance. Those under 17 years of age may not import alcohol or cigarettes. No vaccinations are required.

Currency

The Euro will be introduced in January 2002. Previously, the currency was the Irish Punt (IR£) divided into 100 pence. Approximate exchange rates, which should be used as a guide only, are:

1 Euro = 0.787564 Punt

A$	=	0.45IR£
Can$	=	0.55IR£
S$	=	0.47IR£
UK£	=	1.27IR£
US$	=	0.87IR£

Notes are in denominations of 50, 20, 10 and 5 Punts, and coins are 1 Punt and 50, 20, 10, 5, 2 and 1 Pence. The best rate of exchange is given by Irish banks. Irish currency should be changed back before leaving the country.

Banks ☉open Monday-Friday 10am-12.30pm and 1.30pm-3pm. Most Dublin banks are open until 5pm on Thursdays.

VAT of 15% is added to all goods and services. Cashback is a company that undertakes to refund VAT. Not all stores participate in the scheme. You must have your dockets stamped by customs at your last exit port from the EEC and return the vouchers to Cashback. A fee is charged for this service.

Credit cards are accepted in major stores and hotels.

Telephone

There are public telephones all over the country. International direct dialling is available and the International code is 00, the country code is 353.

Driving

Driving is on the left hand side of the road. The speed limits are as follows.

built up areas - 30mph

single roads   - 60mph

highways   - 70mph

Third party insurance is compulsory.

Miscellaneous

Local Time is Summer Central European Time.

Electricity is 220v AC. As plugs vary it is necessary to purchase an adaptor and a small transformer.

Health insurance is essential. Take any necessary medication with you and a copy of your prescriptions.

Tipping. A 15% service charge is added to hotel and restaurant bills, so no tip is required. Taxi drivers expect 10% and porters usually get 50p per bag.

Dublin

Dublin is compact by international standards, with a population of 952,692. It has wide streets, well designed squares and flower beds down the centre of major roads. Main street O'Connell, has most of the banks, shops and theatres. Dublin is situated on the River Liffey which flows into Dublin Bay.

History

Dublin was mentioned by Ptolemy, a geographer, as a place of note in 140AD. The name "Dublin" comes from the gaelic "Dubhlinn" meaning Black Pool, a more modern title than the Irish name in current use "Baile Atha Cliath", the "Town of the Hurdle Ford". The ancient ford was at the site of the present Father Mathew Bridge.

St Patrick visited Dublin in 448 and converted many of the residents to Christianity. Both the settlement and the religion thrived over the next four hundred years. His feast day is celebrated on the 17th March not only in Ireland, but in also in many countries (Australia, New Zealand, USA, Canada) to which the Irish have migrated either by force or free will.

In 840 a fortress was set up by some Norse sailors as a base, then in 852 a Danish force took possession of the town. Battles between the Irish and the Danes continued until 1014, when the Danes were finally beaten at the Battle of Clontarf.

The English appeared on the scene in 1170, and Strongbow, Earl of Pembroke took control of Dublin. On a visit to view his new acquisition in 1171, Henry II granted Dublin its first charter.

The Irish were never happy with English rule, and the following centuries saw wars between the two, culminating in the Rising of 1916, which took place over the Easter week.

The Irish Free State was established in 1922, but the Civil War that followed saw Dublin once again in the centre of the action.

Dublin has become a cultural centre and a large manufacturing industry has developed. Whiskey distilling, brewing, clothing, glass and food processing are its main industries.

Tourist Information

The Irish Tourist Board has developed a computerised information and reservation system called *Gulliver*. It has stored all major queries including theatres, sport, concerts, places to visit and transport. Gulliver is in all Irish Tourist Information Offices.

Tourist offices are found in Suffolk Street, near Grafton Street/Trinity College, ✆(01) 669 2082, fax 669 2035; Baggot Street; Dun Laoghaire Ferryport; and The Square Tallaght. 24-hour information is available by phoning ✆1-550 11 2233 (58p/min). The website is ⊕www.visit.ie/dublin.

Local Transport

Buses are plentiful and reasonably priced with a flat fare. Cruising taxis are not abundant. The best place to find one is at an hotel or bus station.

Accommodation

A city of commerce, Dublin's hotels are often scratching to fill on weekends as the business traffic declines. Consequently, the astute traveller can often get heavily reduced rates if staying over a weekend, especially out of the larger chain hotels. For more information about Dublin, booking hotels online, and so on, see the official website: ☜www.visitdublin.com

Following is a selection of accommodation with prices for a double room per night, which should be used as a guide only.

Jury's Christchurch Inn, Christchurch Place, Dublin 8, ✆01/454 0000, fax 01/454 0012. Families travelling together will find the one price fits all policy very attractive, with each of the 180 rooms sleeping 3 adults or 2 adults and 2 children and costing the same regardless. A big American chain hotel that offers modern conveniences and comfort right across from Christchurch cathedral - ✪£65.

Northumberland Lodge, 68 Northumberland Road, Ballsbridge, Dublin 4, ✆01/660 5270, fax 01/668 8679. Trinity College is a 15 minute walk away from this pleasant old converted mansion. Spacious and elegant rooms - ✪£70.

Aaronmor House, 1b & c Sandymount Avenue, Dublin 4, ✆01/668 7972, fax 01/668 2377. A large, ramshackle turn of the century house converted to a guest house. Rooms vary in size, but the cramped ones are reasonably cheap - ✪from £50.

Waterloo Lodge, 23 Waterloo Road, Ballsbridge, Dublin 4, ✆01/668 5380, fax 01/668 5786. Located just to the south of the city centre, Waterloo Lodge represents good value for the budget traveller. Rooms are bland but cosy, and a warm, small hotel welcome awaits every guest. A hearty breakfast is included in room rates which are lower out of season or for lengthy stays - ❍£37.50.

Royal Dublin

40 Upper O'Connell Street, Dublin 1, ℂ01/ 873 3666, fax 01/873 3120. Located near Parnell Square in Dublin's north, the Royal Dublin lies in the heart of what might be called the theatre district. A modern lobby, all perfect geometric lines and shapes bleeds off into Georgian sitting rooms complete with frilly cornices, chandeliers and ornate fireplaces. Rooms don't suffer from an identity crisis, however, and are functional, almost chique, modern in design - ❍from £110.

Hotel Conrad Dublin, Earlsfort Terrace 2, Dublin, ℂ(01) 676-5555, fax 676-5424. 191 rooms with private bath. Central, opposite National Concert Hall. Restaurant, bars, pub, parking. Standard room £113-179, Deluxe room ❍£140-190.

Jury's Hotel Dublin, Pembroke Road, Ballsbridge, ℂ(01) 660 5000, fax 829 0400 ✉(travelweb@hotelbook.com(01206). Deluxe hotel in Dublin's most exclusive residential area. 400 rooms, restaurant, bar/ lounge, swimming pool - ❍£135-199.

Trinity Capital Hotel, Tara Street, Dublin, ℂ(01) 648 1000, fax 648 1010. A new hotel situated between the International Financial Services Centre and the Templar Bar District. 80 rooms, restaurant, bar/lounge - ❍£125-150.

Gresham Hotel, O'Connell Street, Dublin, ℂ(01) 874 6881, fax 878 7175 (✉travelweb@hotelbook.com(01529)). A superior 1st class hotel situated in the centre of the city. 288 rooms, restaurant, bar/ lounge, fitness centre - ❍£115-130.

St Stephens Green, Stephens Green, Dublin, ©(01) 607 3600, fax 661 5663 (✎travelweb@hotelbook.com(28983)). A deluxe hotel in the city centre. 75 rooms, restaurant, bar/lounge - ✪£110-240.

The Mont Clare, 74 Marrion Square 2, Dublin, ©(01) 661-6799, fax 661-5663 (✎travelweb@hotelbook.com(13577)). 80 rooms with private bath. Near sightseeing and station. Restaurants, pub, bar - ✪£85-120.

George Frederic Handel Hotel, 16-18 Fishamble Street, Dublin, ©(01) 670 9400, fax 670 9410 (✎travelweb@hotelbook.com(27539)). Situated in the heart of the Temple Bar area. 40 rooms, cafe and bar - ✪£70-140.

Food and Drink

Irish seafood is especially good. Oysters carry the tang of the sea. Brown bread made the way your Grandma made it is the pride of the Irish. Helpings are large.

There is a tourist menu easily recognised by the picture of a chef on the menu cover. These meals are a set price for a three-course meal of simple but good food.

A good selection of wines is available everywhere but it is Guinness and Irish whiskey which are so popular.

The Irish pub is an integral part of Irish lifestyle. It is a gathering place for locals and visitors. Business deals are finalised, family matters discussed, romances conducted and visitors entertained with native wit and song. Every pub has its own charm and clientele. You do not have to drink alcohol to enjoy the lively atmosphere. Many serve coffee and tea and a pub lunch is an economical way to stem the pangs of hunger.

Medieval Banquets are another form of entertainment. Enjoy a wonderful meal and be entertained by musicians, singers and story-tellers. Banquets can be booked prior to departure.

Sightseeing

The city centre has sign-posted walking tours, and this is an excellent way to see the sights. A booklet giving maps and background information is available at the information centre. Fans of James Joyce and his *Ulysses* should make sure they obtain a map that details the positions of the relevant plaques throughout the city.

Take a stroll through **Phoenix Park** which covers 1,760 acres. Within the park stands **Aras an Uachtarain**, the official home of the President. At the entrance to the park is Dublin Zoo founded in 1830.

The **Bank of Ireland** building, in College Green, was constructed between 1729 and 1739 to house the Irish Parliament prior to 1800. The British Government sold the building to the bank in 1802. The showpiece of the building is Pearce's House of Lords with its magnificent Dublin glass chandelier dated 1788. There is also an original masterpiece, the House of Commons Mace.

Trinity College is on the east side of College Green and was built in 1592 on the site of a priory that had been taken over by Henry VIII. The College is the sole constituent college of the university, which was supposed to further the Reformation in Ireland. Covering 40 acres, the College has over 500,000 visitors per year, and the main reason for that is the Library which has the **Book of Kells**, an illustrated manuscript of the Gospels from around the 9th century. Nobody knows where the book was produced, but it is known that in 1007 it was housed at the monastery at Kells, 70km north-west of Dublin. The work is beautifully done, and there are usually two of the four volumes on display at any one time. Although the books are under glass, they are worth seeing. The library is ☉open Mon-Sat 9.30-5pm, Sun 9.30-4.30pm (June-Sept), 12.30-4.30pm (Oct-May).

The **Custom House** on the north bank of the River Liffey is a magnificent building and with the Four Courts is a jewel of Dublin

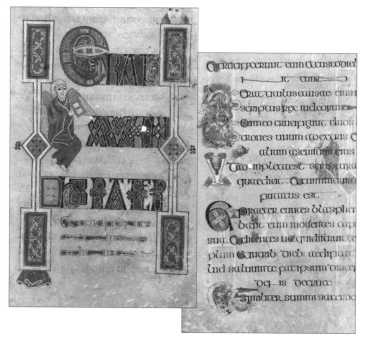

Two pages from the Book of Kells, Trinity College

architecture. It was commenced in 1781 and completed in 1791. It was burnt down in 1921 but has been reconstructed.

Dublin Castle was the centre of English power. The official residence of the Lords Deputy and Lords Lieutenant, the seat of State Councils and sometimes Parliament and the Law Courts. Between 1680-1780 wholesale reconstruction gave us the essence of the form we have today.

The State apartments are approached from the main entrance by the Grand Staircase. A lobby to the left of the landing leads to St Patrick's Hall. Since 1938 it has been the place of inauguration of the President of Ireland. A small piece of trivia about the castle - Bram Stoker, creator of *Dracula*, was once a clerk employed at the castle.

City Hall, adjoining the castle, was erected as the Royal Exchange between 1769-1799. It is a square building in the Corinthian style with three fronts of Portland stone.

Christ Church Cathedral, the Church of Ireland Cathedral, was first built in 1038, and the crypt, containing the grave of Strongbow, survives today. The crypt was opened in the 1930s, and the Earl of Pembroke was discovered to have been a 5 foot 4 inch redhead with broad shoulders. A large part of the church is Gothic Revival.

St Patrick's Cathedral occupies the site of a pre-Norman parish church. It also belongs to the Church of Ireland. A surprising fact for the first time visitor is that there is no Catholic cathedral in Dublin. St Patrick's contains some interesting monuments, among them the grave of Jonathan Swift, Dean of St Patrick's Cathedral 1713-1745. He was the author of *Gulliver's Travels*.

The **General Post Office** is in O'Connell Street, Dublin's main thoroughfare. It was the headquarters of the Irish Volunteers during the 1916 Rising, and it was here that the Republic was announced. There is a series of monuments in the centre of O'Connell Street including the O'Connell Monument, the Parnell Monument and the statue of Father Theobald Mathew.

Opposite Cathedral Street is the **Anna Livia Millennium Fountain**, which the locals call "The Floozie in the Jacuzzi" because that is exactly what it looks like. Anna Livia represents the River Liffey.

Dublin is noted for its theatres. The **Abbey Theatre** is committed to presenting the works of Irish playwrights. The original building was burnt down in 1951 and a new thesatre opened its doors in 1965.

Guinness Brewery is where Ireland's legendary drink is made and it is open to visitors. Enter by the Hop Store, Crane Street.

The **Irish Whiskey Corner**. The Irish invented whiskey. Monks of the 6th and 7th centuries learned the distillation process that had been used in Asia for perfume. They turned it into what they considered a better use! They called it Uisce Beatha, Gaelic for "The Waters of Life". The first licence was granted to Bushills Distillery in 1608 and they are still turning it out. Visitors are welcome but you must phone ✆(01) 725 566 for an appointment.

The **Dublin Literary Pub Crawl** is a three hour entertainment by two actors performing the works of Dublin's famous writers in authentic settings. It starts at Bailey's and continues on to about ten different pubs. Bookings at any local tourist office.

Dublin has many museums, art galleries and libraries all worth seeing if you can spare the time. The **Dublin Experience**, Trinity College, is a multi-media show which traces the history of the city from its earliest times and introduces the visitor to the modern city and its people. The soundtrack includes narration by several voices and the background music has been specially chosen. For those in a hurry, this is your answer.

The Best of Dublin in Brief

Trinity College. Ireland's most prestigious college is over 400 years old. Tours of the campus are available, but not to be missed is the Old Library which contains the famous *Book of Kells*.

Book of Kells. This breathtaking illustrated copy of the Four Gospels, painstakingly completed at the hands of monks in Scotland (this is the most widely-accepted theory), is preserved from the Dark Ages. Its invaluable pages are constantly illuminated and kept under glass for viewing. *College Green, Dublin 2.*

National Museum. This magnificent museum covers 4,000 years of Ireland's history. Highlights are the Viking artifacts and the Tara Brooch from the 8th century. *Kildare Street.*

Dublin Castle. Some of Dublin's oldest architecture is captured in this structure, which was completed in 1220 and was the seat of British rule in Ireland for over 700 years. *Palace Street, Dublin 2.*

Dublin Writers' Museum. A magnificent tribute to the works of many Irish literary greats including Yeats and Joyce. The Georgian mansion in which the museum is located is itself a work of art. *18-19 Parnell Square North, Dublin 1.*

St Patrick's Cathedral. This Church of Ireland cathedral is the longest and oldest in Dublin. Considering the other churches of Europe, you could quite easily give this one a miss. *Patrick's Close, Patrick Street, Dublin 8.*

Dublinia. An exhibition of medieval Dublin featuring displays and a movie presentation. *St. Michael's Hill, Christ Church, Dublin 8.*

Guinness Brewery. For some a visit to Dublin would be incomplete without stopping in at the Guiness brewery, which has been pumping out the thick liquid for more than 240 years. *James's Gate, Dublin 8.*

The Joyce Tower Museum. This tower, the former residence of the famous writer as captured in the opening of *Ulysses*, is a small but extremely informative museum that should spark the interest of James Joyce fans. *Sandycove, Co. Dublin.*

Kilmainham Gaol Historical Museum. A fascinating shrine to the heroes of Irish Independence, those political patriots who endured atrocities inside its walls. *Kilmainham*.

Dublin's Viking Adventure. A lively and involving recreation of a Viking village with re-enactments of Viking life. *Essex Street*.

Grafton Street. An attractive place to shop among the bustle and buskers.

Temple Bar. Dublin's trendy cultural centre for shopping, dining and drinking.

Ceol Interative Irish Music Encounter. People taken by the distinct melodies of traditional Irish music will appreciate this modern approach to recounting every avenue of its history and development.

Cork

Cork, Irish name Corceigh, is the third largest city in Ireland with a population of around 250,000. It is well inland and lies along the banks of the River Lee which in turn flows into natural harbours. The wide main streets contrast with the narrow alleys of the old part of town. Cork is 254km from Dublin.

History
Cork is one of the earliest communities in Ireland. It grew up around a 6th century monastery. The Vikings established the town of Cork as a trading centre in the 900s. An Irish family by the name of McCarthy ruled over the kingdom of Desmond, the region now known as the counties of Cork and Kerry. After the Anglo-Norman invasion, much of the territory was granted to the Fitzgerald family. As Earls of Desmond, they became increasingly Irish.

Cork city remained a centre of English power. In the late 1500s there was an attempted settlement by English colonists. The most famous person to receive land was Sir Walter Raleigh. The Irish attacked the English but lost the battle of Kinsdale in 1601. During the 1600s, Richard Boyle, Earl of Cork became extremely powerful.

Cork became, and still is, a seat of learning. Among writers from Cork are Frank O'Connor, Sean O'Faolain and Somerville and Ross. Famous people who lived there for some time are Edmund Spenser and philosopher George Berkeley.

Today it exports bacon, dairy produce and livestock. It also has a car assembly plant, a brewery and a distillery.

Tourist Information

The Tourist information office is at Tourist House, Grand Parade, Cork, ✆(021) 4271 081, fax 4271 863.

Local Transport

Buses are plentiful but walking is the best way to see this city.

Accommodation

Major credit cards are accepted and prices given are for a double per room per night. Ireland has many bed and breakfasts and so the charge tends is per person per night. All rooms have ensuite, and parking is available. All the places listed are in the city of Cork.

Achill House

Western Road, Cork, ✆021-427 9447, fax 021-427 9447, ✇www.achillhouse.com. A recently renovated guesthouse, with a cosy lounge. The hotel has central heating, which is particularly appreciated during cold Cork winters. - ✪£40 per person per night.

Acorn House, 14 St Patrick's Hill, Cork , ℂ021-450 2474, fax 021-450 2474, ✆www.acornhouse-cork.com. A Georgian guesthouse in the heart of Cork. Highly regarded and comfortable - ✪£20 per person per night.

Crawford House, Western Road, Cork, ℂ021-427 9000, fax 021-427 9927, ✆www.cork-guide.ie/corkcity/crawford-house/welcome.html, email ✉crawford@indigo.ie. 25 rooms. An opulent guesthouse with modern decore and lavish room facilities including en-suites with jacuzzis. Centrally located - ✪£40 per person per night.

Fitzpatrick Silver Springs, Dublin Road, Tivoli, ℂ(021) 507 533, fax 507 641. 100 rooms. Less than 2km from train, 10 minutes from city centre. In spacious grounds. 2 restaurants, bars, gym, squash. Overlooking the River Lee - ✪£70-94.

Metropole, MacCurtain Street 2, ℂ(021) 450 8122, fax 450 6450. 91 rooms most with private facilities. Victorian hotel with new wing added. Very central. Restaurant, bar, parking - ✪£49-79.

Imperial, 14 Pembroke Street, South Mall, ℂ/fax (021) 427 4040. 101 rooms with bath. Historical old world hotel that has been renovated. 3km from car ferry, 230m from train. Dining room, bar, 24 hr room service. Closed Christmas-New Year - ✪£52-121.

The **Youth Hostels** in Cork include the following.
Cork International Youth Hostel, 1 Reddyclyffe, Western Road, ℂ(021) 454 3289, fax 434 3715 - ✪£3.00-6.50.
Sheilas Hostel, Belgrave Place, Wellington Road, ℂ(021) 450 5562, fax 450 0940 - ✪£5.50-10.00.

Many of the pubs in the town and the country have comfortable rooms with breakfast and high tea for a reasonable rate.

Food and Drink

There are plenty of restaurants serving seafood. Try trout, prawns or salmon. There are also excellent steaks, lamb and stews. Don't forget the whiskey and Guinness.

Shopping

There are outstanding bargains available in light tweeds, fine linen, lace, scarves, knitwear, shirts, porcelain and Waterford crystal.

Sightseeing

A trail guide book is available from the information office.

University College was built in 1845 and is part of the National University of Ireland.

St Ann's Shandon Church is famous for its bells. Cork also has Cathedrals, including St Finbar's.

It is the riverside, with its strips of parkland, that makes Cork so attractive. Rest on one of the seats and enjoy the sunset.

Sights Further Afield

The most popular excursion is only five miles from Cork. It is a visit to **Blarney Castle** to attempt to kiss the Blarney stone. The stone is under the battlements and it requires both agility and nerve to attempt this feat. There is nothing between the stone and the ground 26m below. The successful kisser is supposed to be endowed with considerable eloquence. The view from the top of the castle is well worthwhile.

The city of **Waterford**, in the south-east, is where you can see the famous Waterford Crystal being produced, and maybe buy a special souvenir of Ireland.

Dingle Peninsula

A beautiful part of the world, the Dingle Peninsula is Ireland's western-most point. The area has a wealth of sprawling seascapes, medieval buildings, and prehistoric stones, ensuring visitors have plenty to see and appreciate during their stay. The locals are friendly and entertaining - and more than a little obsessed with their resident dolphin, Fungie.

History

Rich in archaelogical history, the soil of the Dingle Peninsula seems to be dense with treasures marking out the eras from 6000 years ago, when hunters and gatherers roamed the land, onwards. Neolithic tombs, stone monuments, gold relics from the Bronze Age, hill forts such as *Cathair Con Ri* from the Iron Age, and more than 30 monastic sites from early christian times have all been discovered.

In the 9th century AD, Vikings established towns and important trade routes in the area, but left no existing remains. They were followed by the Normans who swept through in the 12th century, imposing their influential architecture, social system and culture and bringing the area in line with the rest of their domain.

The Irish language, *Gaeilge*, is still spoken in Dingle, maintaining a link that may be over 2000 years old.

Tourist Information

The tourist information centre of the Dingle Peninsula is *Bord Failte*, in Strand Street, ©066 915 1188. They are ©open 9am-7pm Mon-Sat and 10am-1pm on Sundays between March and October. They are open shorter hours in the off-season.

Accommodation

If you can, you should take advantage of your surroundings in Dingle and book a room with a view. You won't be disappointed. Prices listed below are for a double room per night.

Dingle Skellig Hotel, Dingle, ✆066 9150200, fax 066 9151501. 73 rooms, 42 suites, excellent facilities. On the shores of Dingle Bay with unbeatable views. Blaskets Bar has traditional Irish entertainment - from ☺£80 per person including breakfast.

Heatons Guesthouse, The Wood, Dingle, ✆066 9152288, fax 066 9152324, ✒heatons@iol.ie. 12 comfortable and spacious rooms. Heatons has a superb location on the waterfront, and serves up a wonderful traditional Irish breakfast - B&B ☺IR£25-40 per person.

Barr na Sráide Guesthouse, Upper Main Street, Dingle, ✆66 915 13 31, fax 66 915 14 46. 22 rooms with good facilites. This family-run establishment, located in the heart of Dingle Town, has a fully licensed bar and a homely atmosphere - B&B ☺IR£20-30 per person.

Best of Dingle Peninsula in Brief

Dingle Town. This is the place to stay while you explore the Dingle Peninsula. The harbour provides a stunning vista from your hotel room or while you stroll around its shores. Oceanworld (✆915 2111) is an interesting an informative aquarium. The pub life is superb, with traditional Irish entertainment to sample. And the local dolphin, who lives in the harbour, can be visited on boat trips.

Conor Pass. This narrow road takes you through raw landscapes of soaring cliffs and plunging valleys. At certain points you can look east to Tralee Bay, or west over Dingle Town and out to the Atlantic Ocean.

R559. This coastal road (which you may like to travel by bicycle) will take you in a loop around Europe's westernmost tip. Highlights are Dunbeg Fort, Slea Head and Blasket Island.

Gallarus Oratory. This early Christian church, although 1300 years old, is still in great condition. It resembles an overturned boat and coincidentally manages to keep out the water even today.

Kilmakedar Church. This twelfth century Norman construction is in ruins. Old Latin letters engraved on a stone can be viewed inside. St. Brendan's fifteenth century house is nearby and worth seeing.

Aran Islands

These three limestone islands - Inis Mór, Inis Meáin and Inis Óirr - lie stranded in Galway Bay off the west coast of Ireland. The land is arid, barely tillable, yet somehow the people have managed to withstand the harshness of an environment which seeks desperately to repel them. It seems the remote tranquility of the Arans is the glue that keeps the 1,500 residents firmly attached to their rugged, windswept and beautiful islands.

Tourism is accelerating, which assists a struggling mini-ecomomy. In peak periods, the number of tourists shipped in on day trips from the mainland can outnumber the islanders themselves.

Accommodation

Accommodation on Aran Islands is limited. Below are two options on the main island of Inis Mor, with prices for a double room per night.

Ard Einne Guesthouse, Inis Mor, ✆353 99 61126, fax 353 99 61388, ✉ ardeinne@eircom.net. Well appointed lodgings with a wine license for evening meals. Adequate facilities and good service make it value for money, but don't expect luxury - ☉IR£20 per person for an ensuite.

Doyle's B&B, Lr. Kilronan, Inis Mor, ©353 99 61421. A clean and comfortable B&B that is centrally located, but has very basic facilities and few trimmings - ☉IR£13 per person.

Best of Aran Islands in Brief

Dun Aengus. This fort on Inis Mór should not be missed. Perched above a sheer cliff face with a 60 metre drop, the ancient Celtic fortress has stood for two thousand years overlooking the battering sea which is gradually breaking it apart. Ringed by thick stone walls and a series of spikes, the fortress strikes a powerful defensive poise.

Inis Mór. Other attractions on the largest island are Dún Dubhchath-air, the oldest fort on the Arans, Dún Eochla, the smallest fort but in better condition, and Teampall Bheanain, one of the world's smallest churches, barely 3x2m, now in ancient ruins. Hire a bike when you hop off the ferry.

Inis Meáin. The forts of Dún Chonchúir, a fifth century oval fort with magnificent views, and Dún Fearbhaí, a fourth century square fort, should be visited if you are on the middle island.

Inis Óirr. Two features of the third Aran island are: Caisleán Ui Bhríain, a large castle from the sixteenth century, and the wreck of a cargo ship, the *Plassey*, which can be seen on the rocks. When it was shipwrecked during bad weather in the 1960s, the Aran Islanders ventured into the storm and rescued every single sailor onboard the doomed vessel.

Driving Through Ireland

A Scenic Tour of Ireland by Road

Itinerary - 10 Days - Distance 1610kms

Christ Church Anglican
Cathedral, Dublin

St Patrick's Anglican
Cathedral, Dublin

After exploring **Dublin**, with its historic buildings and atmosphere, head south to **Enniskerry**. The Powerscourt Estate here is well worth a visit. **Glendalough** has ruins of early Christian times. **Arklow** is a popular holiday resort. **Enniscorthy** is the turn-off point to **Rosslare** Ferry terminal, and further south you pass through **New Ross** with its Dutch inspired houses on the way to **Waterford**, of crystal fame.

From Waterford follow the coast through **Youghal**, another popular holiday resort, to **Cork**. Cork is built on the banks of the river Lee. There are many historic buildings to see here. From Cork, head inland to **Blarney Castle**, with its famous stone, and then on to **Glengariff**, a picturesque holiday resort. From here drive north to **Killarney**, where there is much to see and do. Further north of Killarney is **Limerick**, near Shannon Airport. Limerick is a historic place, with many old buildings and castles to see. Driving towards the west coast where you reach **Lahnich**. It is a seaside resort with several golf courses. The road to **Lisdoonvarna** passes along spectacular cliff tops. Lisdoonvarna is well known as a health spa. From here it is a short drive to **Galway**, through **Clarinbridge**, famous for its oysters. Galway is a historic city. Heading northwest from Galway you reach **Clifden** on the coast.

Following the coast you reach **Westport**, which is on Clew Bay. From Westport drive north to **Sligo** with its 13th century church, and **Drumcliffe**, where W.B. Yeats is buried. Further north along the coast you come to **Donegal**, with its castle. This area is home of the Donegal tweed. Take the coastal road to **Dunfanaghy**, which is in the centre of the Gaelic speaking region. Letter-Kenny, south from here, is

Castletown House

county Donegal's main town. Drive south back through Donegal, to **Carrick-on-Shannon**. This route takes you along the banks of **Lough Allen**. Carrick-on-Shannon is known for its fishing and recreation. From here, head back towards Dublin, passing through **Drogheda**. At Drogheda visit the nearby ancient tombs. **Trim** also has ancient monuments worth seeing. Complete your tour back in Dublin.

PART THREE

Index

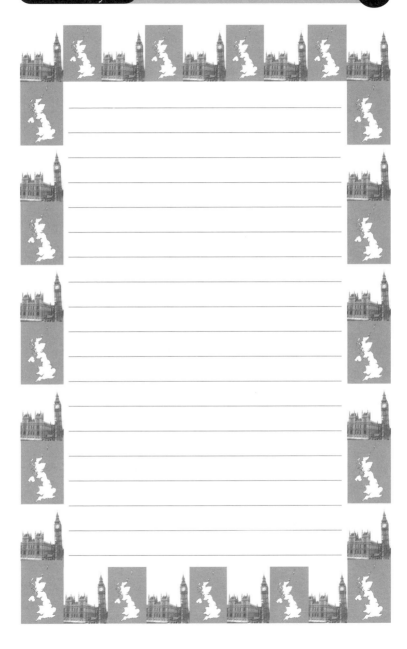